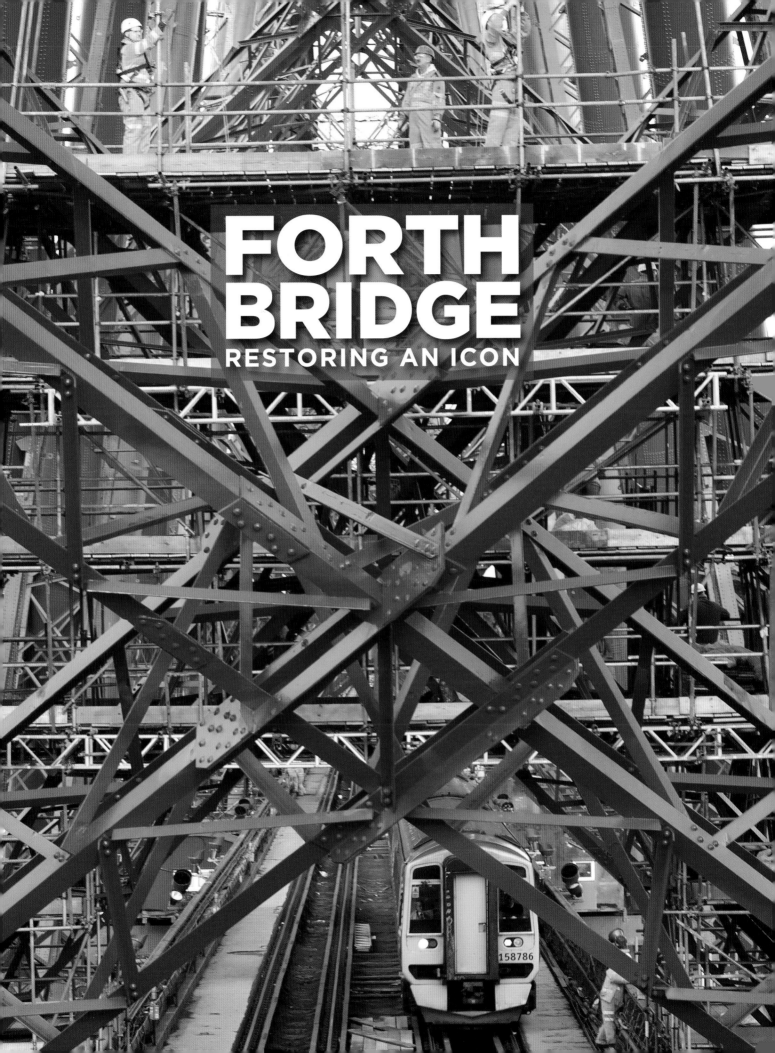

FORTH BRIDGE
RESTORING AN ICON

ISBN: 978-1-907945-19-9

Published by:
Lily Publications Ltd
PO Box 33
Ramsey
Isle of Man
IM99 4LP
Telephone +44 (0) 1624 898446
For and on behalf of Network Rail and Balfour Beatty.

www.lilypublications.co.uk

Typeset in Gotham book and black.

Contents

FORTH BRIDGE FACTS

Work started:	April 1883
Bridge opened:	4 March 1890
Restoration completed:	9 December 2011
Length:	2,467 metres / 8094 ft
Span length:	106.7 metres / 350ft
Main structure (portal to portal):	1,630 metres / 5348 ft
Height of Bridge: High water to top:	110 metres / 361 ft
Rail level: High water to rail:	48.2 metres / 158 ft
Foundation to top:	137 metres / 449 ft
Weight of steel in bridge:	53,000 tonnes / 52,163 tons
Number of rivets:	6.5 million
Concrete and masonry in piers:	120,000 cubic yards faced with 2ft thick granite

Operational information:

Number of trains per day:	200
Number of passengers per year:	3 million

Painting the bridge

Painting area:	255,000 sq metres / 2,744,797 sq ft
Volume of paint used:	240,000 litres / 52,793 gallons
Original paint colour:	Forth Bridge Oxide of Iron
Modern paint colour:	Transgard TG168 better known as 'Forth Bridge Red'

Lighting the bridge

Total number of lights installed:	1,040 lights
Length of cabling required:	35,000 – 40,000 metres / 114,829 – 131,234 ft

Acknowledgements

Produced by:

Written by:
Ann Glen
Craig Bowman
John Andrew
Sara Jayne Donaldson (editor)

Photography:
Cover, title page and photoessay: Kieran Dodds
Historical introduction: Photos courtesy of Glen Collection
Introductions: Photos courtesy of Network Rail and Balfour Beatty

Published by: Lily Publications for and on behalf of Network Rail and Balfour Beatty.

Foreword

Few structures convey the passion, imagination and vision of the Victorian era better than the Forth Bridge. The bridge made a statement of man's intent to overcome every obstacle and, through an artery of railways, to keep the industrial heart of our small island beating.

But to see the Forth Bridge as part of a bygone era is to misunderstand its significance. It is a symbol of fortitude but it is also an integral part of the railway's future. The trains that run upon it are lighter and faster than 120 years ago and the loads are more passengers than freight, but the bridge is as important now as it ever was.

When Network Rail was founded in 2002, the importance of maintaining the Forth Bridge was widely recognised and it was about to undergo the most rigorous renovation in its history.

David Simpson.

Unfortunately, that was not always the case. The 100th anniversary of the structure in 1990 also coincided with a period in the bridge's history when the maintenance regime had been scaled back. Later that decade, when layers of old paint began peeling off, alarm was raised by Queensferry locals, MPs and engineers alike.

A full structural analysis did not consider that the bridge was in risk of failure but it did identify the need to halt the corrosion of steelwork in some exposed areas and identify a new coating system to replace the outdated five-coat method.

Widespread consultation with the paint industry resulted in the recommended use of a glass-flake epoxy paint. The coating system had been used on North Sea oil platforms and was considered to be capable of protecting the bridge from the harsh north European climate.

By 2002, Leighs Paints had been identified as the paint manufacturer of choice and Network Rail entered into a cooperative contract with Balfour Beatty to meet the challenges of restoring the bridge and applying the new coating system.

A solution was required which tackled all the key challenges...

Safety had to be the number one priority. At 110 metres above the fast flowing Firth of Forth, the bridge was a worksite which presented considerable risks. Every inch of the bridge had to be reached, so new methods of access were required.

As a strategically vital rail link carrying over 200 trains a day, the bridge could not be shut except in the early hours of Sunday morning.

Removing paint from the steelwork had to be undertaken in a controlled environment to prevent any of the old lead paint from polluting the estuary below.

And so began a 10 year project which captured the imagination of people across the world. The myth of the never-ending paint job was coming to an end and, over the course of a decade, journalists and TV crews from all corners of the globe reported it.

The full story of the restoration is told in words and pictures through the course of this book, however, the end result, after millions of hours of work, is a bridge that looks as magnificent today as it did when it was opened in 1890.

Although daily passenger numbers crossing the Forth are now greater than at any other time in its history, I'm confident that, should we require it a hundred years from now, the Forth Bridge will still be reaching out across the water, bringing Scotland closer together.

David Simpson
Route Managing Director, Network Rail Scotland

March 2012

The Historical Perspective

The Forth Bridge, the engineering masterpiece *par excellence* of the Victorian age, is acknowledged as one of 'the noble achievements of mankind'. Yet it began in controversial circumstances. A secure passage across the turbulent Firth of Forth was long desired – between 1805 and 1807 a tunnel from South Queensferry to Rosyth was considered then in 1818 there was a proposal for a road bridge. As steam power developed, and railways became major carriers, they had to make do with ferries to take passengers and goods over the estuary. The North British Railway was especially disadvantaged as its network was interrupted by two firths – the Tay and the Forth. This not only lengthened journeys but often the passenger experience was cold, wet and stormy. Increasingly, a rail crossing was seen as essential if the East Coast services, in bitter rivalry with the West Coast companies for 'Scotch traffic', were to prosper.

A 'pinch point' on the Forth, from the Dalmeny shore to the headland at North Queensferry, with the rocky island of Inchgarvie in midstream, seemed a promising location. However, there was a mile and a half of open water to be crossed. After the calamitous collapse of the first Tay Bridge during a winter storm in 1879, confidence was severely shaken and there was much disquiet about large bridges. Although a Forth Bridge Railway Company had been set up in 1873 to take a scheme forward, plans and preliminary work for a suspension bridge between North and South Queensferry were abandoned.

How was a viaduct for a double track railway to be safely taken across the firth? The Railway Board requested a report from three experienced engineers – William Barlow, Thomas Harrison and John Fowler. Through their work with railway companies, they were of the opinion that a suitable durable construction was possible between North and South Queensferry, using Inchgarvie as a stepping stone. It would be the largest railway bridge in the world and an Act of Parliament was obtained in July 1882 for a modified cantilever and girder structure.

In the 1870s, wind pressure for design purposes was assumed to be only 10lbs/ft². Mindful of public anxieties, Parliament now required the Forth Bridge to withstand wind loading of 56lbs/ft², a magnitude unheard of in Britain. Throughout the construction years, wind pressure was monitored as was tidal activity. Furthermore, the Board of Trade made rigorous quarterly inspections of the work in progress.

To carry out the scheme was beyond the means of the North British Railway. Accordingly, the Forth Bridge Railway Company had a joint financial arrangement whereby the North British would contribute 30% of the costs and the Midland Railway 32½% while the North Eastern and Great Northern shared 37½%. Once built, rail traffic and the maintenance of the bridge would be in the hands of the North British.

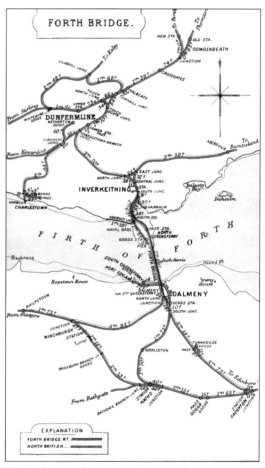

The North British lines around the Firth of Forth, showing the portion owned by the Forth Bridge Railway Company in red.
(The Railway Clearing House 1913)

The demonstration of the cantilever principle, with a Japanese engineering graduate at Glasgow University as the load.
(Glen Collection/*Engineering* 28 Feb 1890)

An extensive site at South Queensferry was laid out for bridge fabrication with rail access and drill roads. (BRB (Residuary) Ltd)

It was John Fowler and his junior partner Benjamin Baker who produced the innovative cantilever design, subsequently demonstrated in a 'human cantilever' image. As cantilevers had never been tried on a structure of such scale, the bridge was at the frontier of technology. The material of which it would be built – steel – was relatively new to the construction industry, indeed, it would be the first structure to use steel made by the Siemens open-hearth process. A special edition of *Engineering* reported:

> *'The choice of material for constructing a bridge of novel design, of extraordinary magnitude, and exposed during erection to the effects of powerful atmospheric disturbances, must have been the subject of much anxious thought and reflection ...'*

Fowler and Baker were justifiably cautious – the structural steel used not only met Admiralty specifications but also those of Lloyd's and other insurers.

Steel had many advantages as it could be bolted, riveted or forged to form the components of a design, and it could be delivered as plates ready for cutting or bending. Above all, it offered engineers a mass produced material of proven strength. To supply the 58,000 tons for the bridge's plates and girders, 65% came from two steel works in Lanarkshire and the balance from South Wales. The rivets, also of steel and amounting to millions, were made in Glasgow.

In January 1883, Tancred, Arrol & Company of Glasgow were appointed contractors for the Forth Bridge. William Arrol was Renfrewshire born in 1839 and largely self-educated. As a young teenager he trained as a blacksmith. Through his interest in engineering, plus his hard work and capacity to innovate, he became a major contractor for bridge works, especially for railways. By 1882, Arrol's company held the contract for the replacement Tay Bridge. Sir Thomas Tancred was a London engineer based at Westminster. By 1886 he had left the Forth Bridge for schemes overseas but usefully he was a member of the London Stock Exchange.

The geology favoured the bridge. An outcome of the Ice Ages was the covering of hard boulder clay on the riverbed through which Inchgarvie's whinstone projected. On either shore, high rocky ground allowed the railway lines to be carried at a sufficient height to allow safe passage for shipping. Surveyors, using an ingenious raft with divers in attendance, set out the centre line of the bridge and the position of its masonry piers using triangulation for the greatest possible accuracy.

Railways were crucial to the project's success. An extension from the station at South Queensferry was taken close to the shore where a large

William Arrol, the energetic and innovative contractor for the Forth Bridge, led a Glasgow company famed for bridges and cranes. (Glen Collection/*Engineering* 28 Feb 1890)

The centre line of the Forth Bridge looking northeast from South Queensferry towards Inchgarvie and the Fife shore in May 1885. Rails on the jetty (right) were accessed from an inclined plane worked by a stationary steam engine. On the left the approach viaduct makes progress. (Glen Collection)

A top junction for tubular columns being assembled in the yard in September 1887. It is said that the Forth Bridge was built twice – once on land and once over the firth. (Glen Collection)

The north approach viaduct nearing full height with the lattice girder for the railway successfully jacked up on top. (Glen Collection)

fabrication yard was set up. Rail access was also made to a yard at North Queensferry. A massive logistical exercise began as sites were prepared and men, materials and machines were gathered. Offices and canteens, hutted living quarters and stores were erected while houses were put up for staff.

Word soon spread about the employment opportunities. Numbers varied as construction advanced with fewer employed in winter than in summer; by July 1887, some 4,500 workers, known as 'briggers', were on site. They came from every part of the British Isles, from the Continent and even from the Far East. With local accommodation full, the North British Railway organised workmen's trains from Edinburgh and from Fife.

Wherever supplies or machines had to be shifted, there were rails in the yards, on the jetties and even on the cantilever tubes. At Inchgarvie and North Queensferry, iron piers were constructed as steam barges and launches brought teams of workmen or materials to sites. As equipment was steam powered, regular supplies of Lothian or Fife coal were essential. Every innovation then known was applied to the management of the project – the telegraph, the new telephone, electric lighting, the latest surveying equipment and the camera all played their part. Engineers had only slide rules to assist their calculations.

With a foundation stone laid, work began in April 1883. The approach viaducts, consisting of ten spans on the south flank and five on the north, were the initial elements to be constructed. In addition, there were four masonry spans on the south side and three on the north. The lattice girders for the viaducts were first built at low level over the line of the masonry piers and gradually raised by jacks. The masonry, of Aberdeen granite, was neatly laid course by course below the steelwork until the desired height of 130ft was reached.

Making the foundations for the cantilever towers was a fraught and strategic phase that took almost three years. It involved the use of caissons – immense wrought iron cylinders 70ft in diameter with a steel cutting edge to submerge into the mud. Each had an inner skin to be loaded with concrete or stone to facilitate sinking to the estuary bed and

A wrought iron caisson on the slipway ready for launching in May 1885. (Glen Collection)

A caisson sunk in position - the interior of No. 3 Caisson at South Queensferry showing the construction of the masonry and concrete fill. Note the lady visitors on the left.
(Glen Collection)

there were temporary timber cofferdams on top. In May 1884 the first caisson was launched from the South Queensferry yard and by September 1885 all were in place, despite one tilting and taking months to be re-floated.

As the estuary bed at South Queensferry was boulder clay, pneumatic caissons, using compressed air, were required; those for the Fife tower were open caissons on rock. At Inchgarvie, two were on boulder clay and two on rock. The pneumatic caissons involved extremely hazardous working conditions up to 90ft below the Forth's surface. Some 7ft beneath a concrete floor, compressed air kept a chamber dry by preventing water seeping in from the firth. Shafts allowed access while air locks maintained air pressure. In this confined space, lit by electric light and using hydraulic shovels designed by Arrol, workmen dug out the hard clay. Like divers, many suffered attacks of agonising 'bends' through gas bubbles forming in their systems.

Once a caisson reached the prescribed depth, the working chamber was filled with concrete and the granite masonry was completed. The installation of steel bedplates for the complex and massive skewbacks then began. Each skewback was the meeting point for five separate cantilever tubes and five box girders. Most upper bedplates allowed for expansion and contraction – the bridge was calculated to move up to 10 inches when temperatures reached 70°F/21°C.

As erecting wooden scaffolding over the firth was impossible, the cantilevers became their own scaffolding – the ease and safety of

A skewback for the Fife cantilever tower showing where the great tubes were secured to the masonry pier. (Glen Collection)

construction was entirely dependent on each portion, once bolted or riveted in place, forming a secure base for further extension. The great tubes of the cantilevers, each 12ft in diameter, rose gradually upwards receiving compression forces while the lattice girders were under tension.

In the yards, machines for bending and dressing steel plate fed drilling machines. These could make ten holes at a time through three layers of metal. Steam cranes shifted prefabricated portions along tracks where rivet holes were tested for alignment. Parts were then marked up and dismantled, a routine ensuring smooth assembly out on the firth.

The enormous cantilever structures grew relentlessly, thanks to men

Briggers working high above the firth on the junction of a tubular member with a girder tie on the Queensferry cantilever in February 1888. (Glen Collection)

The Inchgarvie cantilever in May 1888: a wider structure than its neighbours, this view from the wind gauge shows the congested work site on the small island. A bothy is seen on the rail deck. (Glen Collection)

The developing towers were basically their own scaffolding but here the Fife cantilever bristles with additional timber structures in October 1888. (Glen Collection)

The cantilever towers, seen from the east, were at full height by August 1887, Queen Victoria's Golden Jubilee year. (Glen Collection)

and machines suspended between sea and sky. Two rescue boats were stationed at each cantilever site. Specialist machines had been devised for superstructure work – cranes, hoists, and winches had wire ropes that significantly reduced accidents. Riveting machines enclosed by wire cages were another safety measure. The cantilever arms stretched ever further outwards piece by piece, each side being kept in balance.

It was exposed and dangerous work. The briggers contributed to a 'Sickness and Ambulance Club', which the contractor also supported. This was Victorian industry and there were hundreds of injuries. The number of fatalities was recorded as fifty-seven until recent research revealed six others. Considering the project took eight years in often appalling conditions and that alcohol was a solace, the toll might have been much worse. As Baker sadly observed, such an immense scheme was paid for not only in money but also in lives.

There were twelve hour shifts, even in winter if weather permitted. There was no Sunday work. By night, arc lamps and hundreds of incandescent bulbs provided illumination making an incredible spectacle. By 1887, the year of Queen Victoria's Golden Jubilee, each tower had reached its final height, 361ft above high water mark. Visitors eager to see the 'sublime views' from the cantilever tops and the 'stupendous scale of the works' were welcomed.

The suspended girders spanning the remaining 350ft gaps had then to be closed with sections lifted from barges moored below. By October 1889 it was possible for a director's party to walk from South Queensferry to Fife. Meanwhile, the Forth Bridge Railway Company had constructed the new approach lines from Dalmeny and Inverkeithing, the latter involving perilous rock cutting and tunnelling. In January 1890, two trains of 900 tons each moved slowly side by side along the special bridge rails on the internal viaduct, thereby demonstrating the solidity and successful counterbalancing of the whole colossal structure.

In the yards, every part of the steelwork had been scraped down and coated with boiled linseed oil. The suppliers of paint were Craig & Rose of Leith. The interiors of the cantilever tubes were given one coat of red lead and two coats of white lead paint. After erection, a further coat of the iconic red was applied to the steel – Forth Bridge Oxide of Iron.

Closing the gap between the Inchgarvie (right) and Fife (left) towers with a suspended girder span in November 1889. (Glen Collection)

On 4 March 1890, the Forth Bridge had a royal opening when the Prince of Wales (later King Edward VII) assisted by William Arrol, tightened a rivet with a special key on the north girder span. (Illustrated London News)

A North British train crosses the Forth Bridge from the South Queensferry side in the 1900s. (Glen Collection)

On 4 March 1890 the Prince of Wales (later King Edward VII) officially opened the Forth Bridge by placing a golden rivet on the north girder span. A lavish luncheon followed in the site offices when it was announced that Arrol and Baker would be knighted; John Fowler was made a baronet. The project had cost just over £3million (£235million at 2012 prices).

The Forth Bridge settled into a routine of carrying trains – express and

The centenary of the Forth Bridge in 1990 was celebrated with special trains, organised by the Scottish Railway Preservation Society and hauled by A4 BR No.60009, then named *Osprey*. (Timon Rose)

local, passenger and goods, initially for the North British Railway. It became a visitor attraction to be viewed, travelled over or sailed under. As train weights increased, the internal viaduct was strengthened between 1913 and 1921. After 1923 and the groupings of the private railway companies, the London & North Eastern Railway became the main user. In uncertain times, the bridge stood robust and reassuring with commercial and naval ships passing beneath it. On 16 October 1939 the first aerial attack of the Second World War took place around it.

With nationalisation in 1948, British Railways assumed responsibility. Contrary to popular belief, the Forth Bridge was never painted from end to end. A team of forty briggers armed with scrapers, brushes and paint pots gave weathered areas priority treatment. For access, they had ropes, planks and bosun's chairs. In 1974, the UK government's new safety legislation stopped the cloth-capped 'space walkers' of previous years, making maintenance inevitably more expensive.

By 1964 the Forth Road Bridge had been completed up river and there were adverse comments when the original Forth Bridge had 'rail' coupled to its name. However, in the centenary year of 1990, its unique status was celebrated with special trains, exhibitions and books about its history. Scottish Power installed floodlighting in 1991, thereby enhancing its muscular grace. As a spectacular setting, the Forth Bridge has appeared in films, in adventure stories and in video games.

Meanwhile, British Rail had introduced alkyd paints and shot blasting in 1984. Between 1992 and 1995, the original track system was renewed to enable 180 trains per day to run safely. The Forth Bridge, a key connector in the rail system, was costing £1million a year to maintain. BR announced in 1993 that the painting cycle would be 'interrupted' to save money and the following year, on privatisation, Railtrack took over.

In February 1995, Tam Dalyell, the local Member of Parliament, raised the matter in the House of Commons. At the request of the Health & Safety Executive (HSE), Railtrack began a structural and maintenance assessment. HSE found that maintenance records were unsatisfactory, even non-existent. Investigations showed that in addition to rusting, there was section loss on some secondary members. Although the main structure was secure, deterioration had to be arrested or worse might follow. Improvement notices were served on Railtrack and a £40million refurbishment package began in 1998. On termination of this contract, Railtrack embarked on a new refurbishment strategy and, on the demise of that organisation in 2002, the responsibility for the bridge passed to Network Rail, a not-for-dividend company. Commendably, Network Rail not only continued to support the work on the Forth Bridge but actively increased resources for the project to accelerate its completion.

At the opening in 1890 an engineer was asked, 'How long will the bridge last?' He replied, 'Forever, if you look after it'.

Ann Glen
February 2012

FORTH BRIDGE — G. GAWTHER

LONDON & NORTH EASTERN RAILWAY OF ENGLAND AND SCOTLAND
THE TRACK OF THE FLYING SCOTSMAN

The Forth Bridge became a worthy advertisement for rail travel and a tourist attraction in its own right, as this LNER poster from the 1930s shows. (Glen Collection)

Flaking paint on the Fife cantilever in 2003 shows the need for the comprehensive refurbishment programme that had just begun. (Ann Glen)

The Restoration Challenge

Forth Bridge viewed from North Queensferry following the completion of the restoration works, November 2011.

Example of bridge condition before restoration.

The 9 December 2011 saw the completion of a decade-long project to repair and completely repaint the Forth Bridge for the first time in its 122 years of operation. The restoration works involved one of the largest scale tasks of its kind, featuring innovative scaffolding techniques and encapsulation methods that have since been replicated on other large civil engineering and building projects in the UK and elsewhere. Balfour Beatty, founded only a few years after the bridge's opening, was entrusted with the role of principal contractor for delivery of this unique restoration project on an iconic Scottish landmark. It worked for, and in partnership with, operating customer Network Rail.

PROJECT PLANNING

The scale of the project became evident at the turn of the millennium when Network Rail – having taken over from Railtrack – outlined a set of criteria that stretched well beyond the previous 'care and maintenance' approach. The bridge operator's principal goal was to ensure the Forth Bridge structure remained not only a symbol of engineering excellence but also a fully functioning railway crossing, as fit for purpose as the day it was built.

The project work was undertaken in three principal strands. First, Balfour Beatty had to provide safe access systems for the restoration works which involved innovative scaffolding and encapsulation techniques; second, any corroded steel had to be replaced; and third, the old paint needed to be removed by grit blasting to bare metal, followed by recoating the steelwork with a high-tech three-coat system.

In order to deliver a world-class protective treatment to the bridge, it was fundamental to create robust and often very complex access systems to provide safe working platforms at each and every corner of this unique structure. Balfour Beatty put in place comprehensive procedures and systems to ensure safe and controlled workspaces at all times. This required the construction of an encapsulation system to maintain factory-like conditions for the works to be carried out in a protected environment. At the same time, it had to prevent any contamination of the Firth of Forth by retaining the grit-blasting materials and paints within the enclosures.

The physical work began in 2002 and grew year-on-year as what was effectively a rolling contract moved from one-year to three-year banks of work. These longer-term contracts allowed equipment such as hoists, cranes and accommodation units to be bought outright. New compounds – with offices, welfare facilities, parking, laydown and storage areas – were established at both ends of the bridge; additional storage facilities were then constructed at the base of the Queensferry and Inchgarvie cantilevers. Access routes onto and throughout the bridge, via walkways remote from the permanent way railway line, were installed to provide dedicated 'green zone' separation from the operational railway. In many areas, this involved adding additional elements to the main bridge framework.

WEATHER

The elements posed a constant challenge as the Forth Bridge can experience the weather of all four seasons in one day with conditions changing in a matter of minutes. Supervisors regularly checked that wind speeds were within agreed limits to ensure safe working conditions. When necessary, the scale of the bridge allowed the workforce in exposed locations to be relocated or, in extreme conditions, taken off the bridge and allocated other off-site tasks. Work on the project continued without major disruption throughout an exceptional range of weather conditions, including two of Central Scotland's most prolonged and coldest winters on record.

Minor steel repairs were required to be carried out.

SPECIALIST SKILLS

At the peak of the project, up to 400 tradesmen were employed on a project which would total over 4.5 million working hours. Balfour Beatty formed an Alliance with the four principle subcontractors employed to undertake the works, ThyssenKrupp Palmers, Harsco Infrastructure (SGB), Pyeroy and RBG. Personnel involved included scaffolders, blasters, coaters, material handlers, labourers, plumbers, electricians, fabricators, welders and inspectors; all overseen by a team of experienced engineers, foremen and supervisors. Specialist abseilers were used for running cables and water pipes and painting by hand the 'touch points' which were inaccessible when the major scaffolding assemblies were in place.

Material handlers played a key role in ensuring all resources were at the right place at the right time. Significant movements of material were made by barge to the storage areas constructed at the bases of the Queensferry and Inchgarvie cantilevers. Other major movements of material onto the bridge were made along the railway line from the storage yards at the south side of the bridge during a 'possession window' in the early hours of Sunday mornings, as agreed at an early stage with Network Rail. Between midnight and 8am, as many as 70 material handlers sprang into action utilising hand-push/pull trolleys capable of carrying two tonnes of scaffolding. These crews often moved 120 tonnes of scaffold and other supplies to strategic points on the bridge for the following week's work schedule.

This operation was further enhanced with the use of a road/rail vehicle (RRV) which could both pull rail wagons loaded with the materials required and assist the offload at the designated storage locations. The RRV also assisted the removal of materials and redundant equipment at the end of each shift. The paramount safety demands dictated that operational railway-safety trained supervisors were on duty to control these weekly events and on any other occasion when the specially qualified workforce crossed the railway line to undertake specific tasks. Many of the bridge team worked on this project from its inception through to completion and for many it has become a career-defining experience. These people have come to see the bridge as 'their bridge' and as more than just a place of employment, taking huge pride in what they have contributed to the restoration.

Major logistical storage areas were required with access by barge at Inchgarvie Cantilever.

Complex scaffolds were required to be constructed to access all areas of the bridge.

Scaffold system erected to access areas above track.

SCAFFOLDING

Design and erection of safe systems of access to all areas of the complex bridge structure, whilst also maintaining full operation of the east Coast mainline rail link across the Firth of Forth, were fundamental to the restoration contract. The existing bridge structure was not conceived with a complex maintenance regime in mind and certainly the original designers, Sir John Fowler and Sir Benjamin Baker, together with contractor Sir William Arrol, could not have envisaged the scale of scaffolding systems required to access the bridge over a century after its construction.

At the project outset, Balfour Beatty had to investigate a range of scaffolding options, in consultation with Network Rail, to develop consistently safe systems of access to the full range of scenarios posed by the bridge structure. Exhaustive trials established that traditional tube and fitting scaffolding, supplemented with some 'system scaffolding' at specific locations, provided the best option for the works. Whilst the scaffold systems were then tailor-made to suit their particular application, the design of the existing structure with the similarity in cantilever layout allowed each major scaffold to be repeated a number of times. In turn, the two suspended spans between the Fife and Inchgarvie and between the Inchgarvie and Queensferry cantilevers provided similar repeatability.

The next challenge was posed as the scaffolding could not be assembled and supported as in a normal construction site environment, from the bottom up and to regular geometric principles. Few of the scaffolds were founded on traditional footings but were instead connected to the structure through additional pads and support points welded to the steelwork. Scaffolds were then supported from these points and either built up, constructed from the top down or, in certain circumstances, suspended from steel wire ropes connected to the higher points of the bridge steelwork. Lighter materials were widely introduced to improve weight distribution as on average some 4,000 tonnes of scaffolding was in use on the bridge at any one time. Extensive use of aluminium scaffold tube, both in standard linear form and unit beam configuration, together with the use of recycled plastic scaffold boards on walkways and access routes, in place of traditional timber boards, helped to ease the load.

LOAD MODELLING

At all times during the restoration process, the structural integrity of the bridge was the primary consideration as the weather-resistant plastic membrane could have acted as a 'sail' and created additional wind loads on the structure. Bespoke software was developed by consulting engineers Pell Frischmann. This calculated the additional loading on the bridge via a program which mapped a model of the bridge against the areas of encapsulated scaffolding, by calibrating scaffold weight against wind loads, to ensure the structure was never placed out of balance.

The white encapsulated scaffold was one of the more widely visible features of the project. Hidden behind the safety of the scaffolding and encapsulation the restoration process could take place. Following its erection at each section of the bridge, an initial structural inspection was conducted to assess any repairs or steel replacement required. These inspections found the Victorian steelwork to be in excellent condition. The only repairs and replacement steel required were small angles and minor ties, mainly in areas above the track where generations of steam trains had exhausted steam and smoke which had, over time, corroded the steel sections. Once the steelwork repairs were completed, the main restoration works could commence. The opaque white encapsulation membrane created suspended climatically-controlled 'encapsulation rooms' which optimised light levels and provided the correct environmental conditions. The use of dehumidifiers and diesel-electric heaters ensured a safe and secure working environment without condensation, even when external conditions were far from perfect.

Just as importantly, the residue produced by the blasting process was contained to prevent any contamination of the Firth of Forth below, the external atmosphere or the local area which is home to a number of sensitive environments, including nature reserves, breeding colonies and sites of special scientific interest.

This encapsulation solution has since been employed at Heathrow airport, Sellafield and the neighbouring Forth Road Bridge and has attracted interest internationally from companies undertaking similar projects.

BLASTING AND PAINTING

One of the most extreme jobs of the restoration process was undertaken by blasters wearing protective clothing and helmets. These incorporated a head set with an umbilical cord containing an air line, communication link and power line for tools and lights.

The grit used in the blasting process was a by-product of the copper industry – very hard, but inert. Stored in bulk in the main storage areas at the base of the bridge cantilevers, it was then mixed with air provided by large banks of compressors sited at the north and south compounds. The blasters drew the grit from huge reservoirs at up to 120 psi and fired it onto the structure at up to 200 mph in an operation one experienced and trained worker described as 'like spending the day arm-wrestling'. Within seconds, multiple layers of paint and rust were removed to expose the bare steelwork. Industrial vacuum extractor units then removed the grit and other debris at a rate of up to 20 tonnes of material per hour. Waste was bagged and then moved by barge back to land and onwards to recycling centres and licensed disposal sites. Here the grit was treated, with paint and rust removed for disposal in approved facilities, making the cleansed grit available for re-use.

Finally came the paint, developed specifically for use on the Forth Bridge by Leighs Paints of Bolton, a 150 year old family business which recently became part of global US coatings specialist Sherwin Williams. The three-part coating system originated from the North Sea oil industry where it had been used to protect offshore structures in severe marine environments. Independent trials, conducted by Network Rail and specific to the paints use on the bridge, verified that the topcoat will last for at least 20 years.

The paint system began with a holding primer, containing zinc phosphate to boost its anti-corrosive property, thinly applied at 25-50 microns to the steel by spray techniques. The area was then cleaned down again before a 'stripe coat' of high-build epoxy glass-flake paint was applied by hand to the 6,500,000 rivets and sharp edges of angles and plates to ensure that the specified thickness was achieved. The glass-flake element of the epoxy paint is micronised to give an even surface as the flakes orientate themselves parallel to the surface to give barrier protection and physical reinforcement. The same coating was then progressively sprayed onto the entire 255,000 m² surface to a minimum thickness of 400 microns when cured, having measured a film thickness of 500 microns when wet before solvents are lost as it dries and cures.

Sections of encapsulation on Queensferry Cantilever.

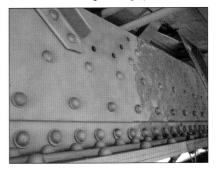

Clean steel following blasting operation.

Finally the trademark topcoat, in the form of 50 microns of 'Forth Bridge Red' paint, was applied – mixed to match the original red oxide colour used in 1890. As the epoxy paint applied in the first two coats does not provide good light resistance, the final coat was of acrylic urethane, giving good colour stability and gloss retention along with an indefinitely recoatable surface to keep preparation to a minimum for future maintenance works. Following inspection and approval of each completed section, the task of dismantling and removing all the scaffolding, encapsulation and support services was systematically undertaken and the rolling restoration programme moved on to the next area.

This pioneering project has used some 240,000 litres of paint to recoat the bridge completely in a single operation for the first time since its construction. Train passengers and the many visitors to the shores of the Forth will now enjoy uninterrupted views of this most photographed of bridges. With the floodlighting system also reinstated as part of the restoration works, the bridge has again regained its reputation as one of Scotland's most recognisable images. It is also important that the bridge looks its best now that it is under consideration for UNESCO World Heritage site status. Whatever the outcome, the use of modern technology now protects this iconic feat of Victorian engineering and much-admired Scottish landmark as the Forth Bridge continues to serve into the 21st century.

John M Andrew, Business Development Director, Balfour Beatty
March 2012

Hand painting some of the 6.5million rivets.

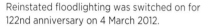

Reinstated floodlighting was switched on for 122nd anniversary on 4 March 2012.

A Unique Workplace

For many of the 1,600 men and handful of women who have worked on the restoration of the Forth Bridge over the last 10 years, this has been a job which has defined our careers. Few of us regarded it as 'just a job'.

The Forth Bridge has symbolism far beyond its functional application as a beast of burden for Scotland's railways. It's a source of national pride, a symbol of man's resourcefulness and, that rarest of things, a beautiful product of an industrial age.

In most jobs, you're happy to see the back of your work at the end of a shift but the Forth Bridge cast a spell on many of us who worked on her or lived near her. For most of us, the Forth Bridge is now 'my bridge'.

Photos and paintings adorn walls, well thumbed books sit on shelves and every news story is followed with unwavering interest. Hundreds of children across Scotland have grown up to know the Forth Bridge simply as 'Daddy's Bridge'.

The knowledge that their time, sweat and skill has contributed to the restoration of such an important structure gives many of those who have worked on this project a sense that their working life has meant something. They have left a legacy – through the bridge, a part of them will live on.

So, completing this project prompts mixed emotions. There's a sense of pride in contributing to a team which has completed such a Herculean task but also a sense of loss in that the community which has existed on the structure for the last 10 years has now moved on.

Undoubtedly the bridge will require ongoing care and attention and, several decades from now, time, tide and North Sea winds will once again demand that the bridge is restored but, for now, we can look back with a sense of achievement.

And when we have cause to drive across the road bridge, not one of us will be able to resist the temptation of glancing eastwards at the glossy red steel without thinking...

'I did that'.

Ian Heigh, Project Manager, Network Rail
March 2012

Ian Heigh.

The
Icon
Restored

Photoessay by Kieran Dodds

A new day dawns at the North Queensferry Bridge Control

23

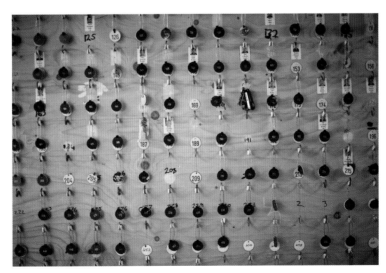

Over a decade, 1,550 men worked on the bridge, with up to 400 employed at any one time at peak periods. Each one was assigned their own tag for safety and identification.

From the South approach, a worker commutes to the bridge along the approach viaduct below the railway track.

In each of the bridge's three cantilever's (Queensferry, Inchgarvie and Fife) bothies provide shelter and welfare facilities for workers.

Men shelter before work in the Inchgarvie bothy.

Wayne Turner and Dale Miller catch up on the news over a morning coffee.

Nearing Inchgarvie on the temporary safe walking route.

Looking down for the access hoist at Inchgarvie.

FORTH RAIL BRIDGE

Discussions at weekly planning/progress meeting

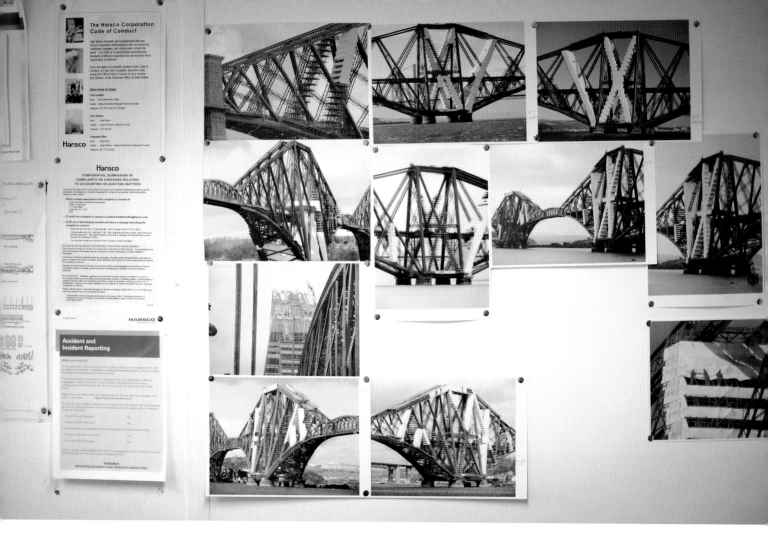

Printouts on the office wall recall peak activity.

Colin 'Big Man/The Big C' Hardie plans a day's work.

Encapsulation (encap) on the lower sections of Inchgarvie.

Alan Gillespie prepares to blast a section of steelwork. The encapsulation ensures consistent conditions and prevents contamination. Blasters used high pressure airlinks to fire grit at the bridge surface at over 200mph. Protective equipment was mandatory for all workers when on the bridge.

Protective blast suits are fitted with personal air supplies.

The cost of paint alone works out at £6 per m². Applying it to the bridge costs £370 per m² due to the challenges involved.

Sprayer John Quinn with his protective suit and mask having applied the paint system. Paint is applied in three layers – a primer, a glass-flake epoxy and a top-coat. The top-coat, which gives the bridge its colour and lustre, is made to match the red-oxide paint first applied over 121 years ago.

The complex structure requires sprayers to be flexible and dynamic in their approach.

Scaffold tubes are stored between the running tracks for removal by the night shift. Over 4,000 tonnes were used at any one time to provide safe access to the bridge.

When the warning klaxon sounds workers at track level halt work and move to a safe position away from the approaching train.

Barrie 'Baza' Donaldson and David 'Robo' Robertson remove scaffold above track level.

55

The maze of steel work viewed
from the safety boat.

Abseiler Johnstone Campbell paints contact points following scaffold removal from the bridge at track level.

Kevin McFarlane paints one of the 6.5 million rivets.

Gordon 'Gudge' Hunter ascends the lower member of Inchgarvie looking towards North Queensferry.

Looking down from track level onto scaffold operations.

Inchgarvie lighthouse stands on a foundation pier for the proposed 'Firth of Forth Bridge', a suspension design abandoned following the Tay Bridge disaster.

William Waddell, in full access gear, prepares to paint contact points on Inchgarvie.

Workers pause to let a
commuter train pass.

Kevin McFarlane enjoys a cup of tea during morning break.

Kenneth Coles takes a break from the hard work with a game of cards.

"I've worked on her for nearly a decade now, I am SO proud that through my own hard work I have written myself into the story of this wonderful structure. I wish we had another ten years, this bridge gets into your blood."

–Colin Hardie, Construction Manager, Balfour Beatty

Gordon 'Gudge' Hunter gathers his equipment from a store room on the bridge.

Inchgarvie island lies in the middle of the Forth.

Abseiling's the only way to reach some areas of the bridge following scaffold dismantle but requires a steady hand.

Abseiler preparing to descend to carry out touch points from the top of the Fife cantilever.

William Waddell negotiates the top member of the Fife Tower, echoing the footsteps of many brave men who have gone before him.

An alimac hoist on the side of Inchgarvie shuttles workers and materials between the different levels.

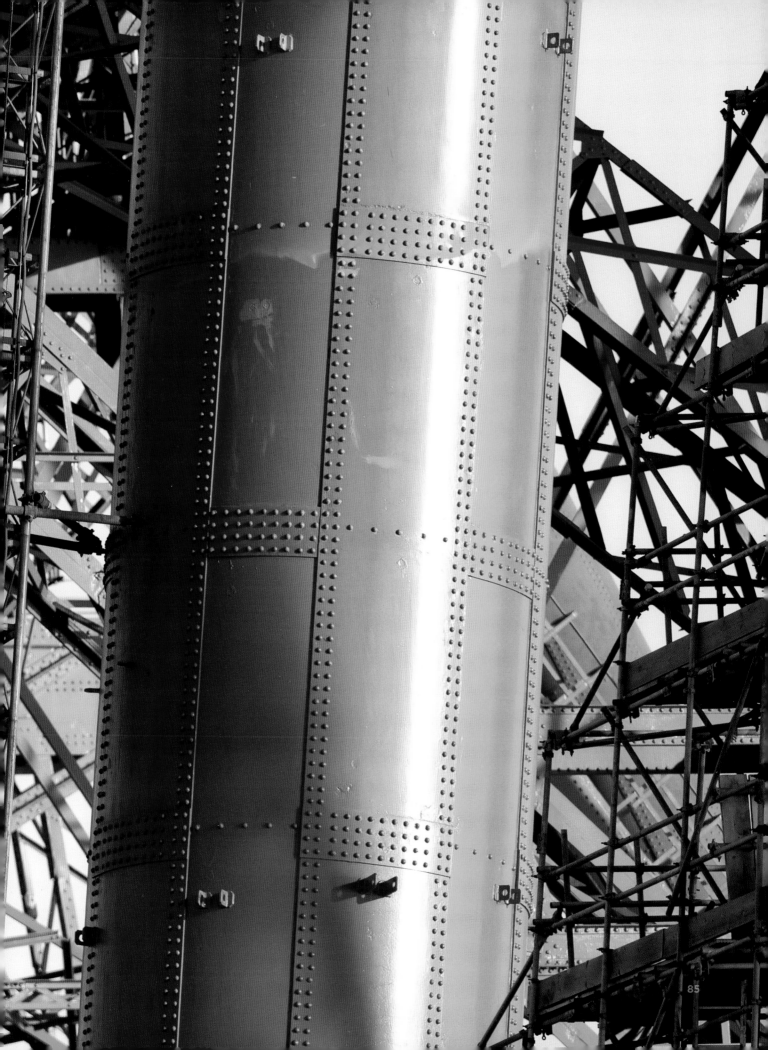

SWL 2000 KG

OPERATOR PLUS 17
PASSENGERS ONLY.
HOIST NOT TO BE
OPERATED IN WIND
SPEEDS IN EXCESS
OF 40MPH.

Hoist operator Neil 'Neily' Louden takes in the sunrise
as the hoist transports workers between levels.

Materials waiting to be moved offsite by road transport

Kenneth Fox in the Fife yard from where materials are moved offsite by road transport.

Working in the Fife yard.

At Inchgarvie, barges move material offsite by sea.

Materials are removed from track side by rail.

A moments peace after a busy shift.

Clocking out at the end of the day.

Workers prepare for the night shift around midnight.

In Dalmeny yard, materials are stored before use.

The night shift walks to the trackside as the wind increases.

Work is undertaken on a 24-hour basis. Saturday night 'possessions' allow unrestricted access to the track when trains are stopped until the early hours of Sunday morning.

Men and materials move onto the bridge via tracks in all conditions, including horizontal rain.

Floodlights focus on activity during the darkness and cold of a winter shift.

Peter 'Pistol' Dunne by Inchgarvie at 3am.

Horizontal rain lashes the men as they load materials onto the road/rail service vehicle.

Looking north along the tracks at Inchgarvie.

John Richardson remains stoical in the face of wind and weather.

66 The worst thing was the cold. It was -15C up on the bridge at one point last year. I had to wear two hoodies and a balaclava."

–David Robinson, Scaffolder

A well earned rest.

The day shift begins again.

Workers access the bridge from the Fife yard in the North and Dalmeny approach in the south.

An alimac hoist descends to the lower levels of Inchgarvie where final work is completed.

Above and overleaf: Synchronised squads of scaffolders pass materials to track side.

Scaffolder
David 'Robo'
Robertson
on the
Queensferry
tower.

Scaffolders perform heroic manoeuvres to remove their complex structures.

The top coat, Transgard TG168, accurately matched to the famous 'Forth Bridge Red'.

> "I'll be sad to finish, working here is something I'll always remember. We blasted tons of paint and rubbish off the bridge to clean the steel so the paint would stick. The views were amazing when you're up on the hoist."
>
> *–Aaron Paddon, Labourer*

Removing his boots, blast sprayer John Quinn finishes another successful shift.

The Contributors

The process of restoring and repainting the Forth Bridge has been an incredible achievement accomplished by thousands of men and women over a ten year period. Only the 'Briggers' that built the Forth Bridge in the 19th century can claim to have shared that sense of accomplishment.

Sadly, no records exist naming all the men, women and children who contributed to building the bridge, so here we are pleased to have captured the names of the modern day 'Briggers' who have contributed to the restoration project over the past ten years. Their dedication and contribution to help safeguard the future of this iconic structure should not be forgotten.

In celebrating the success of this splendid restoration, let us not forget the workers who have passed away during the course of the project, including Robert MacDonald, a popular colleague, who died as a result of a tragic accident on the bridge on 27 January 2010.

NAME, TRADE, COMPANY

C ADAMS, Labourer, Tyssen-Krupp Palmers
C ADAMS, Steelworker, Tyssen-Krupp Palmers
G ADAMSON, Labourer, Tyssen-Krupp Palmers
G ADAMSON, Skipper, Tyssen-Krupp Palmers
R ADIUS, Labourer, Pyeroy
I AIRD, Scaffolder, Tyssen-Krupp Palmers
J AITCHINSON, Labourer, Vital
J AITKEN, Lookout, Orion
C ALEXANDER, Labourer, TEPS
W ALKER, Warden, Vital
A ALLAN, Labourer, MacGregor
J ALLAN, Scaffolder, SGB
K ALLEN, Scaffolder, SGB
S ALLERDICE, Lookout, Orion
S ALLERDIVE, Labourer, Vital
T ALLISON, Labourer, Balfour Beatty
A ANDERSON, Lookout, Vital
A ANDERSON, Planner, Vital
C ANDERSON, Labourer, Vital
I ANDERSON, Blaster, Tyssen-Krupp Palmers
J ANDERSON, Labourer, Vital
J ANDERSON, Scaffolder, SGB
J ANDERSON, Scaffolder, Tyssen-Krupp Palmers
P ANDERSON, Scaffolder, SGB
S ANDERSON, Labourer, Vital
S ANDERSON, Scaffolder,
    Tyssen-Krupp Palmers
J ANDREW, Business Development Director,
    Balfour Beatty
P ANGELINI, Labourer, Vital
H ANJUM, Student Engineer, Balfour Beatty
A ARCHIBALD, Deck Crew, Geckotech
    Solutions Ltd
J ARGUE, Lookout, Orion
R ARIF, COSS, Vital
G ARMSTRONG, EN, SGB
G ARMSTRONG, Lookout, Orion
N ARNOLD, Blaster, Pyeroy
A ASHBURN, Lookout, Orion
C ASHLEY, Warden, Vital
D ASHWORTH, Labourer, Vital
D ASHWORTH, Labourer, Vital
J ASHWORTH, Labourer, Vital
M ASTLE, Coatings Specialist, Scientifics
J AYLES, Labourer, Vital
H AYRES, Scaffolder, Tyssen-Krupp Palmers
R BACKHOUSE, Chief Estimator, Balfour Beatty
S BAILEY, Lookout, Protec
A BAILLIE, Labourer, Vital
S BAILLIE, Painter, Tyssen-Krupp Palmers
A BAIN, Scaffolder, SGB
J BAIN, Scaffolder, SGB
T BAIN, Labourer, Vital
A BAIRD, Scaffolder, Tyssen-Krupp Palmers
D BAIRD, COSS, Vital
H BAIRD, Scaffolder, Tyssen-Krupp Palmers
J BAIRD, EN, SGB
S BAIRD, Labourer, Balfour Beatty
J BALAWTINE, Lookout, Orion
W BARBOUR, Blaster, Balfour Beatty
T BARCLAY, Scaffolder, SGB

A BARKER, Inspector, MacGregors
K BARKEY, Labourer, Vital
L BARKHAM, Scaffolder, SGB
A BARON, Lookout, Scotweld
I BARR, Divisional Managing Director,
    Balfour Beatty.
S BARR, Scaffolder, Tyssen-Krupp Palmers
F BARRETT, Labourer, Tyssen-Krupp Palmers
A BARRIE, Labourer, Vital
W BARRIE, Labourer, Orion
S BARTER, Painter, Tyssen-Krupp Palmers
M BATCHELOR, Supervisor,
    Tyssen-Krupp Palmers
S BATCHEM, Student Engineer, Balfour Beatty
A BEATIE, Labourer, Balfour Beatty
A BEATTIE, Foreman, Balfour Beatty
A BEATTIE, Controller, Vital
A BEATTIE, Scaffolder, Tyssen-Krupp Palmers
J BELL, Deck Crew, Pyeroy
W BELL, Blaster, Pyeroy
N BENNET, Labourer, Vital
P BENSON, Lookout, Orion
A BERNARD, Labourer, Vital
E BERRY, Electrician, Pyeroy
E BERRY, Electrician, Pyeroy
F BERRY, Deck Crew, Pyeroy
J BERRY, Blaster, Pyeroy
J BERRY, Blaster, Tyssen-Krupp Palmers
M BERRY, Labourer, Balfour Beatty
T BIGGINS, Blaster, Pyeroy
D BINNS, Project Engineer, Network Rail
G BIRD, Labourer, Balfour Beatty
K BIRD, Deck Crew, Pyeroy
B BLACK, Scaffolder, Tyssen-Krupp Palmers
B BLACK, Scaffolder, Tyssen-Krupp Palmers
C BLACK, EN, SGB
G BLACK, Blaster, Tyssen-Krupp Palmers
G BLACK, Blaster, Tyssen-Krupp Palmers
I BLACK, Planner, MacGregors
R BLACK, Labourer, MacGregors
R BLACK, Scaffolder, Tyssen-Krupp Palmers
A BLACKHURST, Lookout, Orion
H BLACKWOOD, Scaffolder,
    Tyssen-Krupp Palmers
R BLACKWOOD, Labourer,
    Tyssen-Krupp Palmers
B BLAIR, Lookout, Scotweld
R BLAIR, Lookout, Orion
W BLOUT, Scaffolder, SGB
D BLYTH, Labourer, Charlie O'Donnell
    Construction Ltd
A BOAGEY, Blaster, Pyeroy
A BOAL, Labourer, Vital
M BODYCOMB, Labourer, Balfour Beatty
D BOLLIS, Lookout, Orion
P BOLTON, Lookout, Scotweld
M BONNAR, Scaffolder, SGB
M BONNER, Scaffolder, Tyssen-Krupp Palmers
J BOOTH, Labourer, Tyssen-Krupp Palmers
J BORRETT, Scaffolder, SGB
J BOTHWELL, COSS, Vital
D BOTTOMLEY, Coatings Specialist, WJ Leighs

C BOWMAN, Senior Communications Manager,
    Network Rail
D BOYCE, Senior Communications Manager,
    Network Rail
S BOYCE, Labourer, Vital
I BOYD, Scaffolder, SGB
C BOYLE, Blaster, Tyssen-Krupp Palmers
H BOYLE, Labourer, Balfour Beatty
J BOYLE, Warden, Vital
J BOYLE, Warden, Vital
K BOYLE, Lookout, Vital
S BOYLE, Labourer, Vital
J BOYLE (JNR), COSS, Vital
J BOYLIN, Painter, Vital
W BRADY, Steelworker, Tyssen-Krupp Palmers
S BRAITHWAITTE, Supervisor, Pyeroy
J BRANNAN, Scaffolder, Tyssen-Krupp Palmers
J BRANNEW, Labourer, Vital
J BRANNON, Labourer, Tyssen-Krupp Palmers
R BREEN, Planner, MacGregors
J BRENNAN, Labourer, Balfour Beatty
A BRIAN, COSS, Vital
P BRIAN, Supervisor, Pyeroy
D BRIODY, Commercial Manager,
    Network Rail
G BROCKIE, Labourer, Tyssen-Krupp Palmers
E BROWN, Community Relations Manager,
    Network Rail
J BROWN, Lookout, Scotweld
J BROWN, Scaffolder, SGB
K BROWN, Labourer, Vital
K BROWN, Labourer, Vital
K BROWN, Project Manager, Balfour Beatty
K BROWN, Scaffolder, SGB
R BROWN, Foreman, SGB
R BROWN, Senior Temporary Works Engineer,
    Balfour Beatty
R BROWN, Warden, Vital
S BROWN, Labourer, Vital
S BROWN, Lookout, Scotweld
J BROWNING, Deck Crew, Pyeroy
L BRUMBY, Scaffolder, Tyssen-Krupp Palmers
K BRUNTON, Lookout, Orion
C BRYSON, Labourer, Vital
C BRYSON, Labourer, Vital
D BRYSON, Deck Crew, Pyeroy
T BRYSON, Labourer, Tyssen-Krupp Palmers
T BRYSON, Labourer, Tyssen-Krupp Palmers
T BRYSON, Lookout, Orion
A BURKE, Labourer, Balfour Beatty
T BURKE, Scaffolder, SGB
D BURNS, Blaster, Tyssen-Krupp Palmers
G BURNS, EN, SGB
J BURNS, Labourer, Tyssen-Krupp Palmers
W BURNS, Painter, Tyssen-Krupp Palmers
E BURROWS, Scaffolder, SGB
J BYRNE, Lookout, Scotweld
K BYRNE, Labourer, Balfour Beatty
S CACHLEY, Labourer, Vital
R CADLE, Scaffolder, SGB
J CAIRNS, Office Manager, Balfour Beatty
S CALLAN, COSS, Vital

S CALLAN, Labourer, Vital
J CAMBELL, Labourer, Vital
J CAMBLO, Labourer, Vital
R CAMERON, Lookout, Vital
S CAMERON, Lookout, Orion
G CAMPBELL, Scaffolder, Tyssen-Krupp Palmers
J CAMPBELL, Abseiler, Tyssen-Krupp Palmers
M CAMPBELL, Blaster, Tyssen-Krupp Palmers
M CAMPBELL, Supervisor, Pyeroy
M A CAMPBELL, Deck Crew, Pyeroy
S CAMPBELL, Inspector, Pyeroy
S CAMPBELL, Welder, MacGregor
B CANDLISH, Scaffolder, Tyssen-Krupp Palmers
B CANDLISH, Supervisor, Pyeroy
S CANDLISH, Deck Crew, Pyeroy
S CANDLISH, Labourer, Tyssen-Krupp Palmers
W CANDLISH, Blaster, Tyssen-Krupp Palmers
W CANDLISH, Blaster, Tyssen-Krupp Palmers
S CANTLEY, EN, SGB
D CARGILL, Labourer, Vital
J CARLIN, Lookout, Protec
L CARLIN, Scaffolder, SGB
R CARLIN, Labourer, Vital
R CARLIN, Scaffolder, SGB
T CARLIN, EN, SGB
D CARMICHAEL, Labourer,
    Tyssen-Krupp Palmers
D CARNEGY, Commercial Manager,
    Network Rail
P CARNOCHAN, Labourer,
    Tyssen-Krupp Palmers
G CARR, Labourer, Orion
P CARR, Lookout, Orion
F CARRIE, Scaffolder, SGB
A CARROL, Labourer, Vital
D CARROL, Labourer, Vital
J CARROL, Labourer, Protec
J CARROLL, Blaster, Pyeroy
S CARSELY, Warden, Vital
S CASHLEY, COSS, Vital
K CASSIDY, Scaffolder, Tyssen-Krupp Palmers
S CASSIDY, Blaster, Tyssen-Krupp Palmers
J CATTRELL, Scaffolder, Tyssen-Krupp Palmers
I CAULFIELD, Warden, Vital
D CHALMERS, Deck Crew, Pyeroy
J CHALMERS, Deck Crew, Pyeroy
M CHALMERS, Labourer, Balfour Beatty
P CHALMERS, Labourer, Tyssen-Krupp Palmers
A CHAN, Deck Crew, Geckotech Solutions Ltd
J CHAPMAN, Labourer, Balfour Beatty
D CHARGES, Labourer, Vital
D CHARLES, Lookout, Vital
E CHARNLEY, Labourer, Tyssen-Krupp Palmers
J CHATERS, Blaster, Pyeroy
C CHERRY, Lookout, Scotweld
K CHIESA, Labourer, Vital
G CHILSHOLM, Labourer, Vital
S CHISHOLM, Buyer, Balfour Beatty
C CHISOM, Labourer, Vital
J CHRISTENSEN, Blaster, Pyeroy
A CHRISTIE, Blaster, Tyssen-Krupp Palmers
J CHRISTIE, Lookout, Orion

C CLARK, Secretary, Balfour Beatty
C CLARK, Scaffolder, SGB
D CLARK, Commercial Director, Balfour Beatty
D CLARK, Labourer, Tyssen-Krupp Palmers
G CLARK, Labourer, Tyssen-Krupp Palmers
J CLARK, Lookout, Orion
R CLARK, Scaffolder, Pyeroy
S CLARK, Labourer, Vital
T CLARK, Scaffolder, SGB
S CLARKE, Labourer, Vital
J CLELAND, Labourer, Tyssen-Krupp Palmers
J CLELAND, Warden, Vital
T CLELLAND, Lookout, Scotweld
C COATES, Blaster, Pyeroy
C COATES, Blaster, Pyeroy
C COATES, Blaster, Tyssen-Krupp Palmers
A COCKBURN, Labourer, Tyssen-Krupp Palmers
J COCKBURN, Labourer, Balfour Beatty
A CODE, Blaster, Pyeroy
A CODE, Deck Crew, Geckotech Solutions Ltd
I COGGILL, Labourer, Vital
S COLBORNO, Labourer, Vital
M COLEBOURNE, Scaffolder, SGB
L COLEMAN, Labourer, Vital
K COLES, EN, SGB
S COLLINS, Scaffolder, SGB
T COLLINS, Scaffolder, SGB
S CONNELL, Labourer, Vital
A CONNELLY, Welder, MacGregors
G CONNELLY, Labourer, Tyssen-Krupp Palmers
M CONNETT, Scaffolder, Tyssen-Krupp Palmers
W CONNOLLY, Steelworker, Tyssen-Krupp Palmers
A CONNOR, COSS, Vital
J CONWELL, Warden, Vital
S CONWELL, Labourer, Vital
M COOCHRANE, Scaffolder, SGB
E COOK, Labourer, Vital
L COOK, Labourer, Tyssen-Krupp Palmers
M COOK, Scaffolder, SGB
H CORNS, Steelworker, Tyssen-Krupp Palmers
S COSGROVE, Scaffolder, SGB
M COSTELLO, Labourer, Tyssen-Krupp Palmers
I COULFIELD, Labourer, Vital
W COULSTON, Labourer, Balfour Beatty
S COULTER, Labourer, Vital
D COURT, Labourer, Vital
J COURT, Blaster, Vital
J COUSINS, Assistant Commercial Manager, Network Rail
M COUTTS, Scaffolder, Tyssen-Krupp Palmers
M COWAN, Lookout, Orion
W COWAN, Lookout, Scotweld
W COWAN, Supervisor, Tyssen-Krupp Palmers
G COWIE, Labourer, Vital
S COWIE, Labourer, Vital
J COX, Lookout, Orion
A CRAGGS, Scaffolder, SGB
C CRAIG, Labourer, Tyssen-Krupp Palmers
D CRAIG, Scaffolder, SGB
D CRANSTON, Scaffolder, SGB
D CRANSTON, Scaffolder, SGB
D CRAVEN, COSS, Vital
W CREGGAN, Scaffolder, SGB
C CROOKS, Deck Crew, Pyeroy
C CROOKS, EN, SGB
M CROW, Lookout, Scotweld
A CROWE, Scaffolder, Tyssen-Krupp Palmers
B CROWE, Labourer, Tyssen-Krupp Palmers
A CRUICKSHANK, Steelworker, Tyssen-Krupp Palmers
B CRUICKSHANK, Steelworker, Tyssen-Krupp Palmers
G CRUMLISH, Foreman, Tyssen-Krupp Palmers
P CRUMLISH, Supervisor, Tyssen-Krupp Palmers
S CRUMLISH, Labourer, Tyssen-Krupp Palmers
J CULLEN, Scaffolder, Tyssen-Krupp Palmers
R CUMMING, Blaster, Pyeroy
J CUNNINGHAM, Labourer, Tyssen-Krupp Palmers
S CUNNINGHAM, Lookout, Vital
J CURLEY, Abseiler, Geckotech Solutions Ltd
J CURLEY, COSS, Vital
C CURRAN, Scaffolder, Tyssen-Krupp Palmers
K CURRIE, Scaffolder, SGB
S CURRIE, Controller, AB2000
M CURTIS, Blaster, LINEAR
R CZARNOCKI, Lookout, Orion
N DALZIEL, Blaster, Vital
A DAMSON, Labourer, Tyssen-Krupp Palmers
B DAVIDSON, Deck Crew, Pyeroy
B DAVIDSON, Deck Crew, Geckotech Solutions Ltd
B DAVIDSON, Deck Crew, Pyeroy
J DAVIDSON, Scaffolder, Tyssen-Krupp Palmers
J DAVIDSON, Scaffolder, SGB
S DAVIDSON, Blaster, Pyeroy
J DAVIE, Scaffolder, SGB
J DAVIES, Blaster, Pyeroy
J DAVIES, Supervisor, Pyeroy
M DAVIES, Welder, MacGregors
A DAVIS, Scaffolder, Tyssen-Krupp Palmers
B DAVIS, Labourer, Tyssen-Krupp Palmers
R DAVIS, COSS, Vital
R DAVIS, Labourer, Tyssen-Krupp Palmers
G DAVISON, Scaffolder, Tyssen-Krupp Palmers
J DAWSON, Scaffolder, Tyssen-Krupp Palmers
P DE FRESNED, Deck Crew, Pyeroy
P DE FRESNES, Abseiler, Tyssen-Krupp Palmers
J DEBRAH, Labourer, Balfour Beatty
J DEBROW, Labourer, Balfour Beatty
J DENNIS, Labourer, Vital
S DENNIS, Scaffolder, Tyssen-Krupp Palmers
C DENNY, Foreman, Tyssen-Krupp Palmers
J DENNY, Scaffolder, Tyssen-Krupp Palmers
M DENNY, Scaffolder, Tyssen-Krupp Palmers
M DENNY, Scaffolder, Tyssen-Krupp Palmers
P DEUANTY, Labourer, Vital
B DEVINE, Labourer, Tyssen-Krupp Palmers
D DEVINE, Labourer, Tyssen-Krupp Palmers
F DEVINE, Labourer, Tyssen-Krupp Palmers
C DEVLIN, Labourer, Balfour Beatty
D DEVLINS, Blaster, Pyeroy
A DICK, COSS, Vital
G DICK, Scaffolder, Tyssen-Krupp Palmers
M DICK, Labourer, Vital
M DICK, Scaffolder, Tyssen-Krupp Palmers
A DICKIE, Abseiler, SGB
J DICKSON, Labourer, Vital
S DICKSON, Scaffolder, SGB
T DICKSON, Scaffolder, SGB
R DIXON, Commercial Director, Balfour Beatty
J DOCERTY, Labourer, Vital
J DOCHERTY, COSS, Vital
M DOCHERTY, Lookout, Scotweld
P DODDS, Planner, MacGregors
G DON, Steelworker, Tyssen-Krupp Palmers
B DONALD, Foreman, Tyssen-Krupp Palmers
B DONALDSON, Scaffolder, SGB
G DONALDSON, Scaffolder, Tyssen-Krupp Palmers
M DONLEVY, Lookout, Orion
M DONLEVY, Lookout, Scotweld
J DONNACHIE, Scaffolder, Tyssen-Krupp Palmers
S DONNACHIE, Labourer, Vital
S DONNELL, Scaffolder, SGB
D DONNELLY, Scaffolder, Tyssen-Krupp Palmers
J DONNELLY, Labourer, Vital
J DONNELLY, Scaffolder, Tyssen-Krupp Palmers
M DONNELLY, Deck Crew, Pyeroy
M DONNELY JNR, Deck Crew, Pyeroy
M DOOGAN, Labourer, Vital
S DORAN, Labourer, Pyeroy
A DOUGAY, Scaffolder, SGB
A DOUGLAS, Scaffolder, Pyeroy
M DOUGLAS, Scaffolder, Balfour Beatty
A DOWIE, Labourer, Tyssen-Krupp Palmers
C DOWNIE, Blaster, Pyeroy
C DOWNIN, Deck Crew, Geckotech Solutions Ltd
C DOWNIN, Deck Crew, Pyeroy
P DOYLE, Scaffolder, SGB
K DRUMMOND, EN, SGB
C DRYSDALE, Scaffolder, Tyssen-Krupp Palmers
M DRYSDALE, Scaffolder, SGB
P DUFFY, Warden, Vital
D DUKE, Scaffolder, Pyeroy
P DUNNE, Warden, Vital
A DURDMAN, Labourer, Vital
S DURIE, Trac, Tyssen-Krupp Palmers
S EADIE, Abseiler, Pyeroy
D EASTON, Labourer, Tyssen-Krupp Palmers
W EASTON, Scaffolder, SGB
A EDMISTON, Controller, AB2000
J EDMISTON, Scaffolder, Tyssen-Krupp Palmers
S EDMISTON, Blaster, Tyssen-Krupp Palmers
A EDWARDS, Scaffolder, Tyssen-Krupp Palmers
M EGAN, COSS, Vital
D ELLIOT, COSS, Vital
D ELLIOT, Labourer, Tyssen-Krupp Palmers
M ELLIOT, COSS, Vital
M ELLIOT, Section Engineer, Balfour Beatty
W ELLIOT, Lookout, Orion
S ELLIS, Labourer, Balfour Beatty
W ELLIS, Labourer, Tyssen-Krupp Palmers
A ELLOUISSI, Scaffolder, SGB
J ELLWOOD, Scaffolder, Pyeroy
K ELLWOOD, Scaffolder, Tyssen-Krupp Palmers
D ENNIS ROBETS, Deck Crew, Geckotech Solutions Ltd
A EWING, Labourer, Tyssen-Krupp Palmers
J EWINY, Labourer, Balfour Beatty
J EXRANCE, Blaster, Pyeroy
J EYLES, Labourer, Vital
R FAIRGREIVE, Labourer, Balfour Beatty
N FAIRGRIEVE, Labourer, Charlie O'Donnell Construction Ltd
J FAIRIE, Steelworker, Tyssen-Krupp Palmers
W FAIRLEY, Labourer, Vital
A FALLA, Labourer, Balfour Beatty
T FALLA, Labourer, Balfour Beatty
M FALLIS, Blaster, Pyeroy
T FALLON, COSS, Vital
D FARQUHAR, Labourer, Vital
C FEARNS, Abseiler, Tyssen-Krupp Palmers
B FEARON, Labourer, Vital
C FEARON, COSS, Vital
A FERGUSON, Labourer, Balfour Beatty
D FERGUSON, Lookout, Scotweld
M FERRY, Blaster, Pyeroy
M FERRY, Blaster, Tyssen-Krupp Palmers
C FINDLAY, Blaster, Pyeroy
C FINDLAY, Blaster, Pyeroy
C FINDLAY, Deck Crew, Geckotech Solutions Ltd
G FINDLAY, Steelworker, MacGregors
J FINDLAY, Scaffolder, Tyssen-Krupp Palmers
J FINNEGAN, Steelworker, MacGregors
F FINNEY, Blaster, Tyssen-Krupp Palmers
C FINNIE, Labourer, Vital
D FISHER, Labourer, Tyssen-Krupp Palmers
J FISHER, Scaffolder, Tyssen-Krupp Palmers
P FISHER, Labourer, Tyssen-Krupp Palmers
D FITZPATRICK, Scaffolder, SGB
L FITZPATRICK, Lookout, Scotweld
A FLEMING, COSS, Vital
I FLEMING, Labourer, Tyssen-Krupp Palmers
J FLEMING, Scaffolder, SGB
L FLEMING, Scaffolder, SGB
M FLEMING, COSS, Vital
C FLOCKART, Scaffolder, SGB
A FLYNN, Steelworker, Tyssen-Krupp Palmers
J FLYNN, EN, SGB
C FOLAN, Labourer, Balfour Beatty
J FOLEY, Labourer, Vital
K FOLEY, Scaffolder, Tyssen-Krupp Palmers
S FOOT, Scaffolder, Tyssen-Krupp Palmers
B FORBES, Steelworker, MacGregors
L FORBES, Blaster, Tyssen-Krupp Palmers
J FORD, Labourer, Vital
N FORD, Blaster, Pyeroy
S FORDYCE, Labourer, Balfour Beatty
L FORREST, Scaffolder, SGB
B FORSYTH, Labourer, SGB
T FORSYTH, Labourer, Vital
S FORTHYTH, Labourer, Vital
C FOSTER, Labourer, Vital
D FOSTER, Labourer, Vital
G FOTHERING, Labourer, Tyssen-Krupp Palmers
G FOWLER, Labourer, Vital
A FOX, Labourer, Tyssen-Krupp Palmers
K FOX, Labourer, Tyssen-Krupp Palmers
R FOX, Scaffolder, Pyeroy
W FOX, Labourer, Tyssen-Krupp Palmers
J FOYLAN, Lookout, Orion
M FRAME, Lookout, Vital
D FRASER, Steelworker, Tyssen-Krupp Palmers
J FREUCHER, Labourer, Vital
A FRIEND, Labourer, Tyssen-Krupp Palmers
A FRIEND, Labourer, TEPS
S FROST, Trac, Tyssen-Krupp Palmers
S FULTON, Scaffolder, Tyssen-Krupp Palmers
M FURY, Scaffolder, SGB
P GABEL, Abseiler, Tyssen-Krupp Palmers
P GABEL, Abseiler, Geckotech Solutions Ltd
P GABEL, Deck Crew, Pyeroy
P GABLE, Deck Crew, Geckotech Solutions Ltd
S GAFFNEY, Labourer, Tyssen-Krupp Palmers
J GALLAGER, Labourer, Balfour Beatty
S GALLAGER, Labourer, Vital
K GALLAGHER, Labourer, Vital
D GALLEN, Scaffolder, Tyssen-Krupp Palmers
T GALLEN, Scaffolder, Tyssen-Krupp Palmers
T GALLEN, Scaffolder, SGB
S GALLOWAY, Labourer, Tyssen-Krupp Palmers
J GAMBLE, Labourer, Vital
B GARDINER, Civil Engineer, Network Rail
A GARDNER, Labourer, Balfour Beatty
D GARDNER, Labourer, Vital
H GARDNER, Health & Safety Director, Balfour Beatty
A GASCOIGNE, Metalurgist, Scientifics
C GATER, Blaster, Pyeroy
D GATES, Foreman, Tyssen-Krupp Palmers
D GATES, Labourer, Tyssen-Krupp Palmers
S GEORGE, Steelworker, MacGregors
R GIBB, Labourer, Tyssen-Krupp Palmers
S GIBB, Deck Crew, Pyeroy
A GIBSON, Sub Agent, Balfour Beatty
J GIBSON, Lookout, Orion
R GIBSON, Scaffolder, SGB
W GIBSON, Labourer, Protec
W GIBSON, Storeman, Pyeroy
Y GIBSON, Painter, Tyssen-Krupp Palmers
J GILCHRIST, Scaffolder, SGB
A GILFILLAN, Deck Crew, Pyeroy
G GILLAN, Warden, Vital
A GILLESPIE, Blaster, Pyeroy
G GILMARTIN, Labourer, Vital
G GILMARTIN, Labourer, Tyssen-Krupp Palmers
W GILMORE, Scaffolder, SGB
I GILMOUR, COSS, Balfour Beatty
I GILMOUR, Labourer, Vital
D GILROY, Scaffolder, SGB
G GIVEN, Blaster, Pyeroy
T GLASGOW, Labourer, SGB
S GLEN, Scaffolder, Tyssen-Krupp Palmers
J GODFIELD, Labourer, Vital
S GOMEZ, Sub Agent, Balfour Beatty
A GONSALES, Abseiler, Tyssen-Krupp Palmers
S GOODWEN, Labourer, Vital
D GOODWIN, Labourer, Tyssen-Krupp Palmers
D GORDON, Planner, MacGregors
P GORDON, Scaffolder, SGB
C GOVE, Scaffolder, SGB
A GRAHAM, Blaster, Pyeroy
D GRAHAM, Labourer, Vital
S GRAHAM, Labourer, Tyssen-Krupp Palmers
S GRAHAM, Scaffolder, SGB
W GRAHAM, Scaffolder, SGB
W GRAHAM, Scaffolder, Tyssen-Krupp Palmers
D GRANT, Labourer, Vital
I GRANT, Blaster, Pyeroy
A GRAY, EN, SGB
F GRAY, Lookout, Protec
G GRAY, COSS, Vital
G GRAY, Controller, AB2000
J GRAY, Scaffolder, Tyssen-Krupp Palmers
J GRAY, Scaffolder, Tyssen-Krupp Palmers
K GRAY, Steelworker, MacGregors
P GRAY, EN, SGB
W GRAY, Scaffolder, Tyssen-Krupp Palmers
B GREEN, Scaffolder, Balfour Beatty
S GREEN, Labourer, Tyssen-Krupp Palmers
S GREEN, Administrator, Balfour Beatty
S GREEN, Steelworker, Tyssen-Krupp Palmers
W GREEN, Scaffolder, Tyssen-Krupp Palmers
J GREENHILL, Scaffolder, SGB
C GREER, Abseiler, Geckotech Solutions Ltd
D GRIFFIN, Sub Agent, Balfour Beatty
R GRIFFITHS, Scaffolder, Tyssen-Krupp Palmers
M GRIGGS, Lookout, Orion
J GRUCHALA, Labourer, Balfour Beatty
S GUILFORD, Labourer, Vital
S H CAMPBELL, Deck Crew, Pyeroy
A HADDAN, Scaffolder, SGB
C HAGGERTY, Labourer, Balfour Beatty
J HAGGERTY, Scaffolder, SGB
W HAINING, Painter, Tyssen-Krupp Palmers
G HALAKA, Planning Manager, Balfour Beatty
G HALFORD, Labourer, Vital
W HALFORD, Labourer, Vital
D HALL, EN, SGB
F HALL, Blaster, Pyeroy
J HALL, Labourer, Balfour Beatty
J HALL, Labourer, Vital
W HALLFORD, Labourer, Vital
C HALLIDAY, Blaster, Tyssen-Krupp Palmers
S HALLIWELL, Scaffolder, Pyeroy
D HAMILTON, Labourer, Balfour Beatty
H HAMILTON, Blaster, Tyssen-Krupp Palmers
S HAMILTON, Labourer, Vital
C HANCOCK, Scaffolder, SGB
C HARDIE, Construction Manager, Balfour Beatty
K HARDIE, Blaster, Pyeroy
M HARDIE, Scaffolder, Balfour Beatty
M HARDIE, Worker, SGB
J HARKINS, Scaffolder, Tyssen-Krupp Palmers
S HARPER, Labourer, Vital
J HARRISON, Scaffolder, SGB
K HARROWER, Labourer, Tyssen-Krupp Palmers
R HARROWER, Supervisor, Tyssen-Krupp Palmers
J HART, Labourer, Balfour Beatty
C HASTIE, Lookout, Orion
T HAUGHEY, Labourer, Vital
J HAUGLIAN, Labourer, SGB
L HAVLIN, Lookout, Orion
J HAWKSHAW, Lookout, Orion
D HAY, Scaffolder, SGB
P HEALY, Scaffolder, Tyssen-Krupp Palmers
W HEALY, Lookout, Orion
I HEEPS, Blaster, Pyeroy

H HEGGARTY, Scaffolder, Tyssen-Krupp Palmers
I HEIGH, Project Manager, Network Rail
J HENDRY, Labourer, Balfour Beatty
P HERLIHY, Labourer, Vital
P HERLIHY, Scaffolder, Tyssen-Krupp Palmers
D HETHRINGTON, Scaffolder, SGB
B HEWITT, Scaffolder, SGB
K HICKEY, Labourer, TEPS
W HIDDLESTON, Labourer, Balfour Beatty
S HIGGINS, Scaffolder, Tyssen-Krupp Palmers
J HILL, Scaffolder, Tyssen-Krupp Palmers
T HILL, Scaffolder, SGB
S HILLIER, Scaffolder, SGB
C HILLOCK, Labourer, Vital
C HILLVER, Labourer, Vital
A HOGG, Labourer, Vital
R HOLDING, Labourer, Tyssen-Krupp Palmers
R HOLMES, Scaffolder, SGB
M HOOPER, Communications Manager, Balfour Beatty
G HOPE, Environmental Manager, Balfour Beatty
G HORRIBINE, EN, SGB
I HOSEY, Labourer, Balfour Beatty
H HOWARTH, Scaffolder, SGB
H HOWARTH, Scaffolder, SGB
H HOWARTH, Scaffolder, SGB
M HOWIE, Lookout, Scotweld
A HUGHES, Lookout, Scotweld
D HUGHES, Labourer, Tyssen-Krupp Palmers
D HUGHES, Labourer, Tyssen-Krupp Palmers
J HUGHES, Electrician, Balfour Beatty
M HUGHES, Scaffolder, Tyssen-Krupp Palmers
M HUGHES, Scaffolder, Tyssen-Krupp Palmers
B HUME, Heath & Safety Manager, Balfour Beatty
D HUNTER, Lookout, Scotweld
D HUNTER, Senior Commercial Manager, Network Rail
G HUNTER, Abseiler, Tyssen-Krupp Palmers
G HUNTER, Scaffolder, Tyssen-Krupp Palmers
I HUNTER, EN, SGB
M HUNTER, QA Engineer, Balfour Beatty
W HUNTER, Lookout, Orion
G HURLBERT, Scaffolder, Tyssen-Krupp Palmers
S HUTCH, Labourer, Balfour Beatty
A HUTCHINSON, Labourer, Tyssen-Krupp Palmers
S HUTCHINSON, Lookout, Orion
D HUTCHISON, Scaffolder, Tyssen-Krupp Palmers
N HUTCHISON, Scaffolder, Tyssen-Krupp Palmers
N HUTCHISON, Scaffolder, Tyssen-Krupp Palmers
A HUTTON, Scaffolder, SGB
G HUTTON, Abseiler, Tyssen-Krupp Palmers
M HYATT, Project Manager, Balfour Beatty
J HYND, Labourer, Vital
P HYND, Blaster, Pyeroy
P HYND, Blaster, Tyssen-Krupp Palmers
T INGLIS, Steelworker, Tyssen-Krupp Palmers
D INGRAM, Foreman, Balfour Beatty
M INGRAM, Deck Crew, Pyeroy
G INNES, Labourer, Balfour Beatty
J IRELAND, Labourer, Vital
I IRONS, COSS, Vital
T IRONS, Deck Crew, Pyeroy
A IRVINE, Labourer, Vital
D IRVINE, Labourer, Balfour Beatty
D IRVINE, Steelworker, Tyssen-Krupp Palmers
D IRVINE, Steelworker, Tyssen-Krupp Palmers
D IRVINE, Steelworker, Tyssen-Krupp Palmers
J IRVINE, Labourer, Balfour Beatty
J IRVINE, Scaffolder, SGB
H IVORS, Labourer, Tyssen-Krupp Palmers
D J ELLIOT, Scaffolder, Tyssen-Krupp Palmers
B JACKSON, Foreman, Balfour Beatty
D JACKSON, Scaffolder, SGB
L JACKSON, Labourer, Tyssen-Krupp Palmers
W JACKSON, Scaffolder, Tyssen-Krupp Palmers
G JAMES, Labourer, SGB
S JAMES, Scaffolder, SGB
D JAMIESON, EN, SGB
R JARRETT, Labourer, Vital
R JEFFREY, Labourer, Vital
R JEFFRIES, EN, SGB
D JENKINS, Planner, MacGregors
S JENKINS, Scaffolder, Pyeroy
I JEWEL, Labourer, Tyssen-Krupp Palmers
J JOBSON, Abseiler, Tyssen-Krupp Palmers
G JOHN, Labourer, Balfour Beatty
C JOHNSON, Deck Crew, Geckotech Solutions Ltd
T JOHNSON, Scaffolder, SGB
B JOHNSTON, Scaffolder, SGB
G JOHNSTON, Lookout, Scotweld

J JOHNSTON, Lookout, Scotweld
L JOHNSTON, Labourer, MacGregors
T JOHNSTON, Lookout, Scotweld
A JOHNSTONE, Blaster, Pyeroy
J JOHNSTONE, COSS, Protec
F JOLLY, Labourer, Balfour Beatty
C JONES, Labourer, SGB
G JONES, Labourer, Vital
I JONES, Rope Access Examiner, Pell Frischmann
M JONES, Scaffolder, SGB
G JONSTON, Lookout, Orion
R JUDE, Lookout, Scotweld
S KALIN, Labourer, Vital
A KANE, Scaffolder, SGB
D KARDACH, Labourer, Tyssen-Krupp Palmers
D KARDACH, Labourer, Balfour Beatty
D KARDASH, Scaffolder, Tyssen-Krupp Palmers
T KARTAL, Scaffolder, SGB
S KAY, Labourer, Tyssen-Krupp Palmers
P KAYS, COSS, Vital
D KEARNEY, COSS, Vital
J KEENAN, Scaffolder, Tyssen-Krupp Palmers
B KELLY, Plater, MacGregors
F KELLY, Section Engineer, Balfour Beatty
J KELLY, Lookout, Orion
S KELLY, Scaffolder, Tyssen-Krupp Palmers
A KENNEDY, Scaffolder, SGB
C KENNEDY, Labourer, Pyeroy
D KENNEDY, Labourer, Tyssen-Krupp Palmers
D KENNEDY, Plater, MacGregors
J KENNEDY, Inspector, MacGregors
S KENNEDY, Labourer, Vital
B KENNY, Deck Crew, Pyeroy
S KEOGH, Scaffolder, Tyssen-Krupp Palmers
K KEOUGH, Lookout, Orion
G KER, Labourer, Tyssen-Krupp Palmers
T KERBER, Scaffolder, SGB
D KERR, Labourer, Vital
D KERR, Scaffolder, SGB
G KERR, Chief Estimator, Balfour Beatty
J KERR, Labourer, Vital
M KERR, Labourer, SGB
S KERR, Labourer, Tyssen-Krupp Palmers
G KERRIGAN, Supervisor, Tyssen-Krupp Palmers
R KIDD, Scaffolder, SGB
B KILGOUR, Scaffolder, Tyssen-Krupp Palmers
C KILGOUR, Abseiler, Tyssen-Krupp Palmers
A KILPATRICK, Labourer, Tyssen-Krupp Palmers
C KING, Deck Crew, Pyeroy
J KING, Electrician, Vital
J KING, Lookout, Scotweld
J KING, Steelworker, Tyssen-Krupp Palmers
P KING, Scaffolder, Pyeroy
B KINNELL, Worker, SGB
D KIRBY, Abseiler, Geckotech Solutions Ltd
D KIRK, Labourer, Tyssen-Krupp Palmers
J KIRKPATRICK, Labourer, Tyssen-Krupp Palmers
P KIRTLAN, Supervisor, Pyeroy
D KNIGHT, Scaffolder, Pyeroy
A KNOX, Scaffolder, Vital
C KNOX, Labourer, Vital
G KNOX, Labourer, Vital
J KNOX, Scaffolder, SGB
A KRASNISI, Labourer, Vital
D KRZYZANOWSKI, Plater, MacGregors
W KUCHARSKI, Labourer, Tyssen-Krupp Palmers
G LAFFERTY, Lookout, Orion
D LAIDIER, Painter, Tyssen-Krupp Palmers
A LAIDLAW, Labourer, Balfour Beatty
A LAIDLAW, Lookout, Scotweld
J LAING, Labourer, Vital
K LAING, Inspector, Pyeroy
A LAIRD, Senior Programme Commercial Manager, Network Rail
B LAIRD, Lookout, Scotweld
D LAIRD, Labourer, Tyssen-Krupp Palmers
D LAMB, Scaffolder, SGB
I LAMOND, Labourer, Protec
S LAMONT, Labourer, Tyssen-Krupp Palmers
J LAND, Project Engineer, Pell Frischmann
J LANG, Labourer, Balfour Beatty
D LANGTON, Scaffolder, Tyssen-Krupp Palmers
D LAVERICK, Blaster, Pyeroy
P LAWLOR, Labourer, Tyssen-Krupp Palmers
D LAWRIE, Scaffolder, Tyssen-Krupp Palmers
J LAWRIE, Planner, MacGregors
T LAWRIE, Lookout, Protec
J LEES, Scaffolder, SGB
R LESNER, Blaster, Pyeroy
B LETHAM, EN, SGB
A LI MACKENZIE, Steelworker, MacGregors
D LIDDELL, Blaster, Pyeroy
S LINDSAY, Labourer, Tyssen-Krupp Palmers
J LITTLE, Scaffolder, SGB

P LITTLE, Scaffolder, SGB
D LITTLEJOHN, Scaffolder, SGB
J LONGLEY, Labourer, Tyssen-Krupp Palmers
S LONGMIRE, COSS, Vital
F LONIE, Planner, MacGregors
K LORIMER, Scaffolder, Balfour Beatty
K LORIMER, Scaffolder, Tyssen-Krupp Palmers
R LORIMER, Scaffolder, SGB
A LOTHIAN, Scaffolder, SGB
N LOUDEN, Labourer, Tyssen-Krupp Palmers
A LOVE, Steelworker, Tyssen-Krupp Palmers
S LOVEL, Scaffolder, SGB
J LOVELL, Labourer, SGB
G LOWE, Foreman, Balfour Beatty
J LUMSDEN, Labourer, Tyssen-Krupp Palmers
G LUPTON, EN, SGB
R LYNCH, Scaffolder, SGB
C LYNN, Scaffolder, Tyssen-Krupp Palmers
P MACALISTER, Labourer, Vital
J MACARTHUR, Sub Agent, Balfour Beatty
D MACDLEOD, Scaffolder, SGB
J MACDONALD, I Corr Coatings Inspector, Pell Frischmann
C MACDOUGAL, Labourer, Protec
A MACFARLANE, Labourer, Tyssen-Krupp Palmers
A MACGONIGLE, Abseiler, Pyeroy
D MACHSER, COSS, Vital
A MACINTOSH, Steelworker, MacGregors
L MACINTYRE, Inspector, Pyeroy
S MACINTYRE, Scaffolder, SGB
A MACKAY, Labourer, Vital
M MACKAY, Planner, MacGregors
D MACKENZIE, Plater, MacGregors
I MACKIE, Blaster, Pyeroy
D MACKIN, Labourer, Tyssen-Krupp Palmers
C MACKINNON, Student QS, Balfour Beatty
J MACLENNAN, Welder, MacGregors
J MACLENNAN, Welder, MacGregors
C MACLEOD, Scaffolder, SGB
D MACLEOD, Scaffolder, Balfour Beatty
E MACLEOD, Inspector, MacGregors
J MACLEOD, COSS, Vital
D MACQUARRIE, Labourer, Vital
R MACRAULAY, Labourer, SGB
P MAGEE, Scaffolder, Tyssen-Krupp Palmers
W MAHER, Labourer, Vital
S MAIDEN, Inspector, Pyeroy
J MAIN, Labourer, Balfour Beatty
D MAIR, Head of Contracts & Procurement [Asset], Network Rail
K MAJOR, Steelworker, MacGregors
C MALLON, Handler, Tyssen-Krupp Palmers
D MANDERS, Lookout, Orion
M MANN, Deck Crew, Pyeroy
G MANSELL, Planning Assistant, Balfour Beatty
R MARLES, Blaster, Pyeroy
F MARS, Supervisor, Vital
A MARSHALL, Blaster, Tyssen-Krupp Palmers
B MARSHALL, Trainee QS, Balfour Beatty
C MARSHALL, Labourer, Vital
F MARSHALL, Lookout, Orion
I MARSHALL, Labourer, Vital
J MARSHALL, Labourer, Vital
M MARSHALL, Labourer, Tyssen-Krupp Palmers
N MARSHALL, Welder, MacGregors
P MARSHALLP, Scaffolder, SGB
R MARSHALLR, Labourer, SGB
A MARTIN, Labourer, Tyssen-Krupp Palmers
A MARTIN, Planner, MacGregors
B MARTIN, COSS, Vital
D MARTIN, Lookout, Orion
D MARTIN, Scaffolder, Tyssen-Krupp Palmers
J MARTIN, Works Superintendent, Balfour Beatty
P MARTIN, Deck Crew, Pyeroy
R MARTIN, Lookout, Orion
W MARTIN, Inspector, Pyeroy
L MARTINDALE, Purchasing Manager, Balfour Beatty
J MASSON, Lookout, Orion
S MASSON, Abseiler, Tyssen-Krupp Palmers
J MASTERSTON, Scaffolder, SGB
J MASTERTON, Scaffolder, SGB
J MASTERTON, Scaffolder, SGB
H MAWDSLEY, Painter, Tyssen-Krupp Palmers
S MAWDSLEY, Scaffolder, Tyssen-Krupp Palmers
W MAWDSLEY, Labourer, Tyssen-Krupp Palmers
A MAXWELL, Labourer, Vital
S MAXWELL, Scaffolder, Tyssen-Krupp Palmers
E MAZS, Document Controller, Balfour Beatty
A MCABENY, COSS, Vital
G MCALGAS, Labourer, Vital
D MCALLISTER, Labourer, Vital
P MCALLISTER, EN, SGB

W MCARRON, Labourer, Vital
T MCATEER, Planner, MacGregors
G MCAULAY, Labourer, Vital
J MCBRIDE, COSS, Vital
R MCBRIDE, Deck Crew, Pyeroy
M MCCABE, EN, SGB
M MCCABE, Scaffolder, Balfour Beatty
R MCCAIG, Lookout, Scotweld
D MCCALL, Labourer, Vital
J MCCALL, Deck Crew, Pyeroy
J MCCALL, Scaffolder, SGB
J MCCALL, Scaffolder, Tyssen-Krupp Palmers
D MCCALLUM, Blaster, Pyeroy
B MCCARRON, Labourer, Vital
W MCCARRON, Supervisor, Vital
R MCCAUSLAND, Scaffolder, SGB
W MCCLAREN, COSS, Vital
W MCCLUCKIE, Lookout, Protec
J MCCLUNE, Handler, Tyssen-Krupp Palmers
A MCCONNACHIE, Supervisor, Tyssen-Krupp Palmers
P MCCORMACK, Scaffolder, SGB
W MCCORMICK, Labourer, Vital
C MCCOURT, EN, SGB
A MCCRACKEN, COSS, Vital
D MCCREADY, Labourer, Tyssen-Krupp Palmers
D MCCREADY, Labourer, Tyssen-Krupp Palmers
G MCCREADY, Labourer, Tyssen-Krupp Palmers
G MCCREADY, Labourer, Tyssen-Krupp Palmers
D MCCRUMB, Labourer, Tyssen-Krupp Palmers
N MCCULLOCH, COSS, Vital
R MCCULLOCH, COSS, Vital
R MCCUTCHEON, Labourer, Vital
J MCDADE, COSS, Vital
N MCDADE, COSS, Vital
P MCDADE, Scaffolder, Tyssen-Krupp Palmers
P MCDAID, Scaffolder, SGB
A MCDONALD, Lookout, Vital
D MCDONALD, Scaffolder, SGB
D MCDONALD, Scaffolder, SGB
G MCDONALD, Labourer, Balfour Beatty
I MCDONALD, Scaffolder, Tyssen-Krupp Palmers
I MCDONALD, Scaffolder, SGB
K MCDONALD, Scaffolder, SGB
K MCDONALD, Scaffolder, SGB
M MCDONALD, Planner, Vital
P MCDONALD, Scaffolder, SGB
R MCDONALD, Blaster, Tyssen-Krupp Palmers
R MCDONALD, Painter, Tyssen-Krupp Palmers
S MCDONALD, Labourer, Balfour Beatty
S MCDONALD, Labourer, Vital
S MCDONALD, Scaffolder, Tyssen-Krupp Palmers
C MCDOUGALL, EN, SGB
D MCDOWALL, Labourer, Tyssen-Krupp Palmers
D MCDOWALL, Labourer, Tyssen-Krupp Palmers
R MCDOWELL, Lookout, Orion
J MCEWAN, Scaffolder, SGB
J MCEWAN, Scaffolder, Tyssen-Krupp Palmers
A MCFADIAN, Foreman, Tyssen-Krupp Palmers
A MCFADYEN, Scaffolder, Tyssen-Krupp Palmers
B MCFADYEN, Scaffolder, Tyssen-Krupp Palmers
I MCFADYEN, Planner, MacGregors
R MCFADYEN, Scaffolder, Tyssen-Krupp Palmers
B MCFADYON, Labourer, Tyssen-Krupp Palmers
J MCFARLANE, Deck Crew, Geckotech Solutions Ltd
K MCFARLANE, Deck Crew, Pyeroy
J MCFARLINE, Labourer, Vital
R MCGEE, Labourer, Vital
T MCGEE, Labourer, Balfour Beatty
T MCGEE, Scaffolder, SGB
J MCGHEE, Scaffolder, Balfour Beatty
G MCGIBBON, Scaffolder, SGB
A MCGILL, Labourer, Vital
H MCGILL, Labourer, Tyssen-Krupp Palmers
J MCGILL, Labourer, Tyssen-Krupp Palmers
J MCGILL, Labourer, Balfour Beatty
M MCGILL, Lookout, Vital
J MCGINLAY, Blaster, Tyssen-Krupp Palmers
C MCGINLEY, Blaster, Tyssen-Krupp Palmers
J MCGINLEY, Blaster, Pyeroy
G MCGINTY, Worker, SGB
M MCGONIGLE, Labourer, SGB
G MCGOWAN, Scaffolder, SGB
J MCGOWAN, Labourer, Tyssen-Krupp Palmers
L MCGOWAN, Blaster, Pyeroy
L MCGOWAN, Blaster, Pyeroy
L MCGOWAN, Painter, Tyssen-Krupp Palmers
I MCGREGOR, Labourer, Balfour Beatty
B MCGUIGAN, Scaffolder, Tyssen-Krupp Palmers
A MCGUINNESS, Blaster, Pyeroy
C MCGURK, Labourer, Vital
J MCGURN, Scaffolder, Tyssen-Krupp Palmers

G MCHOHAN, COSS, Vital
P MCILDOON, Deck Crew, Pyeroy
A MCINNES, Scaffolder, Tyssen-Krupp Palmers
T MCINNES, Office Manager, Balfour Beatty
T MCINNES, EN, SGB
I MCINTOSH, Commercial Manager,
    Network Rail
S MCINTOSH, Labourer, Vital
D MCIVER, Scaffolder, SGB
M MCIVER, Scaffolder, SGB
A MCIVOR, Scaffolder, Tyssen-Krupp Palmers
C MCIVOR, Scaffolder, Tyssen-Krupp Palmers
A MCKAY, Labourer, Vital
A MCKAY, Lookout, Orion
D MCKAY, Lookout, Orion
T MCKAY, Labourer, Tyssen-Krupp Palmers
W MCKAY, COSS, Vital
M MCKELVIE, Scaffolder, SGB
M MCKEND, Labourer, Balfour Beatty
D MCKENNA, Lookout, Orion
J MCKENNA, Labourer, Balfour Beatty
K MCKENZIE, Lookout, Orion
S MCKENZIE, Scaffolder, Tyssen-Krupp Palmers
N MCKEOWN, Scaffolder, Tyssen-Krupp Palmers
J MCKFARLANE, Deck Crew, Pyeroy
J MCKINNON, Deck Crew, Pyeroy
J MCLAREN, Labourer, Vital
S MCLAREN, Labourer, Tyssen-Krupp Palmers
S MCLAREN, Sub Agent, Balfour Beatty
D MCLAUGHLIN, Blaster, Pyeroy
J MCLAUGHLIN, Labourer,
    Tyssen-Krupp Palmers
J MCLAUGHLIN, Labourer, TEPS
J MCLAUGHLIN, Scaffolder, SGB
J MCLAUGHLIN, Scaffolder,
    Tyssen-Krupp Palmers
K MCLAUGHLLN, Labourer,
    Tyssen-Krupp Palmers
J MCLAY, Scaffolder, SGB
W MCLAY, Labourer, Vital
N MCLEAN, EN, SGB
R MCLEAN, Steelworker, MacGregors
S MCLEAN, Scaffolder, SGB
E MCLEARY, Labourer, Vital
A MCLENNON, Labourer, Vital
N MCLEOD, Painter, Tyssen-Krupp Palmers
S MCLEOD, Labourer, Vital
M MCMAHON, Labourer, Tyssen-Krupp Palmers
M MCMAHON, Scaffolder, Tyssen-Krupp Palmers
M MCMANUS, Labourer, Vital
R MCMANUS, Labourer, Vital
R MCMANUS, Labourer, Vital
S MCMARTH, Scaffolder, SGB
G MCMASTER, Painter, Vital
S MCMATH, Scaffolder, SGB
A MCMILLAN, Trac, SGB
C MCMILLAN, Labourer, Balfour Beatty
R MCMILLAN, COSS, Vital
D MCMONAGLE, Blaster, Pyeroy
D MCMONAGLE, Scaffolder, SGB
M MCMULLAN, Labourer, Tyssen-Krupp Palmers
F MCMULLEN, Labourer, Tyssen-Krupp Palmers
W MCMULLEN, Labourer, Tyssen-Krupp Palmers
B MCMURRAY, Labourer, Vital
P MCNALLY, Labourer, Tyssen-Krupp Palmers
E MCNEIL, Lookout, Scotweld
M MCNEIL, Lookout, Orion
M MCNEIL, Steelworker, MacGregors
A MCNEILL, Deck Crew, Pyeroy
F MCNEILL, Blaster, Pyeroy
S MCNEILL, Scaffolder, Tyssen-Krupp Palmers
G MCPHAIL, Lookout, Orion
J MCPHAIL, Lookout, Orion
M MCPHEE, Labourer, Vital
G MCPHERSON, Labourer,
    Tyssen-Krupp Palmers
K MCQUADE, Labourer, Vital
P MCQUADE, Scaffolder, SGB
P MCQUADE, Scaffolder, Tyssen-Krupp Palmers
T MCQUILTER, Lookout, Orion
E MCVEY, Labourer, Vital
S MEADE, Labourer, Vital
A MEARNS, Labourer, Vital
R MEECHAN, Scaffolder, SGB
S MEIKLE, Scaffolder, SGB
G MELDRUM, Painter, Tyssen-Krupp Palmers
P MELVILLE, Painter, Tyssen-Krupp Palmers
R MENZIES, Lookout, Scotweld
A MERTON, Scaffolder, Pyeroy
M MESSE, Labourer, Balfour Beatty
A MILLER, Foreman, SGB
B MILLER, Blaster, Tyssen-Krupp Palmers
D MILLER, Scaffolder, SGB
K MILLER, Head of Construction Management,
    Network Rail
P MILLER, EN, SGB
W MILLER, Lookout, Orion

D MITCHELL, Lookout, Orion
J MITCHELL, Lookout, Vital
J MITCHELL, Scaffolder, SGB
L MITCHELL, Labourer, Tyssen-Krupp Palmers
P MITCHELL, Scaffolder, SGB
P MITCHELL, Scaffolder, SGB
S MITCHELL, Scaffolder, SGB
C MLAY, Lookout, Scotweld
G MOFFAT, COSS, Vital
J MOFFAT, COSS, Vital
J MOFFAT, Labourer, Vital
W MOFFAT, Labourer, Protec
C MOIR, Planner, MacGregors
S MOIR, Scaffolder, Balfour Beatty
J MONAGHAN, Labourer, Vital
S MONAGHAN, COSS, Vital
S MONGHAN, Labourer, Vital
J MONTAGUE, Crane Driveriver, Vital
I MONTGOMERY, Labourer, MacGregors
S MONTGOMERY, Labourer, Vital
V MONTGOMERY, Labourer, Vital
V MONTGOMERY, Scaffolder, SGB
W MONTGOMERY, Warden, Vital
A MOODY, Scaffolder, Pyeroy
T MOODY, Scaffolder, Pyeroy
J MOOHAN, Scaffolder, Tyssen-Krupp Palmers
J MOOHAN, Worker, Balfour Beatty
B MOON, Labourer, Tyssen-Krupp Palmers
I MOONEY, Steelworker, Tyssen-Krupp Palmers
J MOONEY, Scaffolder, Pyeroy
M MOONEY, Scaffolder, SGB
D MOORE, Scaffolder, SGB
J MOORE, Scaffolder, SGB
P MOORE, Lookout, Orion
D MORAN, Lookout, Scotweld
I MORAN, Labourer, Tyssen-Krupp Palmers
A MORGAN, Scaffolder, SGB
B MORGAN, Scaffolder, SGB
C MORGAN, Labourer, Vital
S MORGAN, Lookout, Scotweld
J MORRIS, Scaffolder, SGB
A MORRISON, Labourer, Protec
A MORRISON, Labourer, Vital
D MORRISON, Office Manager, Balfour Beatty
I MORRISON, Plater, MacGregors
K MORRISON, Scaffolder, Pyeroy
M MORRISON, Scaffolder, Tyssen-Krupp Palmers
R MORRISON, Scaffolder, SGB
W MORTON, Scaffolder, Tyssen-Krupp Palmers
D MUIR, Labourer, SGB
D MUIR, Labourer, Tyssen-Krupp Palmers
D MUIR, Painter, Tyssen-Krupp Palmers
M MUIR, Painter, Tyssen-Krupp Palmers
R MUIR, Scaffolder, Tyssen-Krupp Palmers
R MUIR, Supervisor, Tyssen-Krupp Palmers
W MUIR, Labourer, Tyssen-Krupp Palmers
A MUIRHEAD, Labourer, Balfour Beatty
C MULLEN, COSS, Vital
C MULLEN, Scaffolder, Tyssen-Krupp Palmers
S MULLIGAN, Lookout, Orion
A MUNRO, Blaster, Pyeroy
A MUNRO, Blaster, Tyssen-Krupp Palmers
A MUNRO, Blaster, Pyeroy
D MUNRO, Lookout, Orion
G MUNRO, Labourer, SGB
G MUNRO, Lookout, Orion
J MUNRO, Labourer, Tyssen-Krupp Palmers
J MUNRO, Lookout, Scotweld
J MUNRO, Scaffolder, SGB
R MUNRO, Scaffolder, Tyssen-Krupp Palmers
R MURDOCH, Labourer, Vital
S MURDOCH, COSS, Vital
J MURDOCK, Warden, Vital
D MURPHY, Scaffolder, Tyssen-Krupp Palmers
R MURPHY, Deck Crew, Pyeroy
J MURRAY, Warden, Vital
P MURRAY, Safety Adviser, Balfour Beatty
S MURRAY, Abseiler, Geckotech Solutions Ltd
J MURRAY (JNR), Labourer, Vital
M MYA, EN, SGB
A MYALL, Scaffolder, Tyssen-Krupp Palmers
A NEALON, Deck Crew, Pyeroy
J NEARY, EN, SGB
W NEELY, Scaffolder, Tyssen-Krupp Palmers
W NEELY, Scaffolder, Tyssen-Krupp Palmers
A NEILSON, Painter, Tyssen-Krupp Palmers
B NELSON, Labourer, Tyssen-Krupp Palmers
G NELSON, Labourer, Vital
S NELSON, Controller, AB2000
S NELSON, Welder, MacGregors
S NESBITT, Project Manager, Balfour Beatty
D NESS, Scaffolder, SGB
E NEWBIGGING, Blaster, Pyeroy
G NEWBIGGING, Labourer, Balfour Beatty
G NEWBIGGING JNR, Labourer, Balfour Beatty
P NEWELL, Scaffolder, SGB
A WYLIE, Steelworker, MacGregors

A NICHOLSON, Labourer, Balfour Beatty
T NICOL, Lookout, Scotweld
B NICOLSON, Planner, MacGregors
C NIMMO, Blaster, Pyeroy
C NIMMO, Blaster, Tyssen-Krupp Palmers
M NOBLE, Lookout, Orion
P NOHAR, COSS, Vital
R NORMAN, Steelworker, MacGregors
L NORMAND, Abseiler, Tyssen-Krupp Palmers
O NORMAND, Blaster, Pyeroy
G NORRIE, EN, SGB
A OAG, Steelworker, MacGregors
A O'BOYLE, Labourer, Vital
M O'BRIEN, Labourer, Tyssen-Krupp Palmers
G O'DONNELL, Labourer, Tyssen-Krupp Palmers
G O'DONNELL, Labourer, TEPS
J O'DONNELL, Labourer, Vital
M O'FLASHERTY, Scaffolder, SGB
E OGILVIE, Lookout, Scotweld
D OHARA, Scaffolder, Tyssen-Krupp Palmers
J O'HARA, Blaster, Tyssen-Krupp Palmers
J OHN RICHARDSON, Labourer, Vital
C OLIN SMITH, Labourer, Vital
R OLIPHANT, Blaster, Pyeroy
R OLIPHANT, Blaster, Pyeroy
R OLIPHANT, Deck Crew, Geckotech
    Solutions Ltd
A OLIVER, Project Manager, Balfour Beatty
K OMAR, Blaster, Pyeroy
D ONEIL, Lookout, Scotweld
I ONEIL, Lookout, Scotweld
B O'NEIL, Blaster, Tyssen-Krupp Palmers
B O'NEIL, Labourer, Balfour Beatty
R O'NEILL, Scaffolder, Tyssen-Krupp Palmers
J ORDON HALL, Labourer, Balfour Beatty
C O'REILLY, Labourer, Vital
B ORMISTON, Lookout, Scotweld
M OSBORNE, Scaffolder, SGB
M OSBORNE, Scaffolder, SGB
M OSBORNE, Scaffolder, SGB
P OSBORNE, Scaffolder, SGB
P OSBORNE, Scaffolder, SGB
T OSBORNE, Scaffolder, SGB
J OSEPH SHIELS, Blaster, Pyeroy
G OWEN, Labourer, Vital
A PADDON, Labourer, Balfour Beatty
K PAGET, Scaffolder, SGB
M PALMER, Labourer, Vital
D PANTON, Labourer, Tyssen-Krupp Palmers
J PANTONY, QS, Balfour Beatty
J PARK, Scaffolder, SGB
R PARKER, Labourer, Tyssen-Krupp Palmers
B PARSONS, Trainee QS, Balfour Beatty
H PATERSON, Foreman, Tyssen-Krupp Palmers
S PATERSON, Scaffolder, Tyssen-Krupp Palmers
S PATERSON, Scaffolder, SGB
W PATERSON, Scaffolder, SGB
T PATISON, Lookout, Orion
A PATON, Labourer, SGB
A PATON, Lookout, Orion
D PATON, Labourer, Tyssen-Krupp Palmers
M PATTERSON, Labourer, Balfour Beatty
M PATTERSON, Steelworker,
    Tyssen-Krupp Palmers
W PATTERSON, Labourer, Vital
J PATTIE, Labourer, Tyssen-Krupp Palmers
T PATTISON JNR, Lookout, Orion
D PAWSON, Scaffolder, SGB
R PEARCE, Labourer, Balfour Beatty
S PEARSON, Blaster, Pyeroy
W PEARSON, Welder, MacGregors
C PENMAN, QS, Balfour Beatty
S PENMAN, Scaffolder, Tyssen-Krupp Palmers
A PENNYCUICK, Deck Crew, Pyeroy
D PENNYCUICK, Foreman, Balfour Beatty
D PENNYCUICK, Nightshift Supervisor,
    Balfour Beatty
A PENNYCUIK, Deck Crew,
    Geckotech Solutions Ltd
D PERRY, Technical Services Director,
    Balfour Beatty
D PETERS, Lookout, Scotweld
J PETIT, Deck Crew, Pyeroy
I PETKOV, Scaffolder, SGB
J PETTET, Abseiler, Tyssen-Krupp Palmers
D PHEBY, Director, Pell Frischmann
D PHILIPS, Labourer, SGB
A PIERO, Labourer, Vital
J POJDA, Labourer, Tyssen-Krupp Palmers
J POJDA, Labourer, Balfour Beatty
E POTTER, Blaster, Pyeroy
J POTTINGER, Scaffolder, SGB
S POWELL, Blaster, Tyssen-Krupp Palmers
C PRATT, Access Supervisor, Balfour Beatty
A PRICE, Scaffolder, SGB
S PRINGLE, Labourer, Vital

C PRITCHARD, Labourer, Tyssen-Krupp Palmers
G PROCTER, COSS, Vital
C PROCTOR, COSS, Vital
F PROTOR, Painter, Tyssen-Krupp Palmers
F PRYDE, Scaffolder, SGB
P PRYDE, Scaffolder, SGB
C PUNTON, Lookout, Orion
W PURCELL, Scaffolder, SGB
R PURDIE, COSS, Vital
B PURDY, Labourer, Vital
J QUEEN, Labourer, SGB
W QUEEN, Lookout, Orion
S QUIGLEY, Lookout, Orion
J QUINN, Blaster, Tyssen-Krupp Palmers
J QUINN, Blaster, Pyeroy
B RAE, Blaster, Pyeroy
G RAEBURN, Scaffolder, SGB
B RAIN HARDING, Lookout, Scotweld
K RAINEY, Labourer, Tyssen-Krupp Palmers
J RAMP, Labourer, Vital
J RAMSAY, Labourer, Orion
J RAMSAY, Labourer, Vital
J RAMSAY, Scaffolder, Tyssen-Krupp Palmers
C RANKIN, Scaffolder, Tyssen-Krupp Palmers
W RATCLIFF, Labourer, SGB
A RAY, Deck Crew, Pyeroy
A REA, Deck Crew, Geckotech Solutions Ltd
L REA, Temporary Works Engineer,
    Balfour Beatty
G REID, Labourer, Tyssen-Krupp Palmers
J REID, Blaster, Pyeroy
M REID, Safety Adviser, Balfour Beatty
R REID, Lookout, Scotweld
S REID, Labourer, Balfour Beatty
S REID, Scaffolder, Tyssen-Krupp Palmers
S REID, Scaffolder, Tyssen-Krupp Palmers
T REID, Abseiler, Tyssen-Krupp Palmers
T REID, Blaster, Pyeroy
J REILLY, Lookout, Scotweld
J RENNIE, Scaffolder, SGB
R RENNIE, Operations Director, Balfour Beatty
W RENNIE, Deck Crew, Pyeroy
G REYNOLDS, Planner, MacGregors
R REYNOLDS, COSS, Vital
R REYNOLDS, Labourer, Vital
P RHODES, Abseiler, Tyssen-Krupp Palmers
P RHODES, Deck Crew, Geckotech Solutions Ltd
R RHODES, Deck Crew, Pyeroy
S RICH, Scaffolder, SGB
T RICHARD, Labourer, Vital
A RICHARDSON, COSS, Vital
D RICHARDSON, Labourer, Vital
G RICHARDSON, Labourer, Vital
H RICHARDSON, Warden, Vital
H RICHARDSON, Planner, MacGregors
J RICHARDSON, Safety Adviser,
    Balfour Beatty
J RICHARDSON, Warden, Vital
M RICHARDSON, Handler,
    Tyssen-Krupp Palmers
P RICHARDSON, Labourer,
    Tyssen-Krupp Palmers
P RICHARDSON, Labourer,
    Tyssen-Krupp Palmers
S RICHARDSON, Labourer, Balfour Beatty
S RICHARDSON, Controller, Vital
T RICHARDSON, Labourer, Vital
T RICHARDSON, Labourer, Vital
D RICHARDSON JNR, COSS, Vital
J RICHARDSON JNR, COSS, Vital
J RICHARSON, Warden, Vital
B RIDDEL, Scaffolder, SGB
E RIDDELL, Blaster, Pyeroy
G RIDDELL, Abseiler, Pyeroy
E RIDDLE, Painter, Tyssen-Krupp Palmers
B RISHARDSON, Planner, MacGregors
J RITCHIE, Blaster, Tyssen-Krupp Palmers
C ROBB, Planner, MacGregors
A ROBERT, Scaffolder, Tyssen-Krupp Palmers
D ROBERT, Deck Crew, Pyeroy
C ROBERTS, Steelworker, MacGregors
D ROBERTS, Blaster, Pyeroy
D ROBERTS, Labourer, Vital
J ROBERTS, COSS, Vital
J ROBERTS, Labourer, Balfour Beatty
R ROBERTS, Abseiler, Tyssen-Krupp Palmers
R ROBERTS, Abseiler, Geckotech Solutions Ltd
R ROBERTS, Deck Crew, Pyeroy
A ROBERTSON, COSS, Vital
B ROBERTSON, Blaster, Tyssen-Krupp Palmers
B ROBERTSON, Painter, Tyssen-Krupp Palmers
D ROBERTSON, Scaffolder, SGB
G ROBERTSON, Painter, Tyssen-Krupp Palmers
J ROBERTSON, Scaffolder, Tyssen-Krupp Palmers
K ROBERTSON, Lookout, Orion
K ROBERTSON, Labourer, Vital
L ROBERTSON, Blaster, Pyeroy

L ROBERTSON, Scaffolder,
    Tyssen-Krupp Palmers
R ROBERTSON, Labourer, Vital
K ROBSON, Scaffolder, Pyeroy
L ROBSON, Scaffolder, SGB
D RODGER, Labourer, Tyssen-Krupp Palmers
C RODGERS, Lookout, Protec
D ROGERS, Labourer, Vital
J ROLLO, Blaster, Tyssen-Krupp Palmers
M RONSON, Scaffolder, SGB
T RONXIN, Scaffolder, SGB
K RONY, Scaffolder, SGB
J ROONEY, Lookout, Orion
A ROSE, Welder, MacGregors
L ROSOLEK, Labourer, Tyssen-Krupp Palmers
L ROSOLEK, Labourer, Balfour Beatty
L ROSOLEK, Labourer, Tyssen-Krupp Palmers
D ROSS, Lookout, Orion
I ROSS, Labourer, Tyssen-Krupp Palmers
J ROSS, Scaffolder, Tyssen-Krupp Palmers
P ROSS, Labourer, Vital
R ROSS, Deck Crew, Pyeroy
S ROXBURGH, Scaffolder, SGB
P RUSSEL, Lookout, Scotweld
D RUSSELL, Plater, MacGregors
S RUSSELL, Labourer, Vital
S RUSSELL, Labourer, Vital
G RYAN, Blaster, LINEAR
B RYAN ADAMS, Labourer, Balfour Beatty
A SALMOND, Scaffolder, SGB
S SALMOND, Deck Crew, Pyeroy
S SALMOND, Painter, Tyssen-Krupp Palmers
T SANDERSON, Scaffolder, SGB
I SANDS, Warden, Vital
J SCANIAN, Labourer, Vital
D SCANLAN, Lookout, Vital
G SCANLAN, Labourer, Vital
J SCANLON, Labourer, Vital
K SCANLON, Welder, MacGregors
J SCAWLAW, Scaffolder, SGB
J SCOTLAND, Labourer, Vital
A SCOTT, Construction Manager, Balfour Beatty
D SCOTT, EN, SGB
J SCOTT, Abseiler, Pyeroy
J SCOTT, Lookout, Orion
M SCOTT, Managing Director, Balfour Beatty
P SCOTT, Foreman, SGB
R SCOTT, Scaffolder, Pyeroy
R SCOTT, Scaffolder, Tyssen-Krupp Palmers
R SCOTT, Scaffolder, Tyssen-Krupp Palmers
T SCOTT, Foreman, SGB
P SCOTTJNR, Scaffolder, SGB
S SCULLION, Labourer, Tyssen-Krupp Palmers
J SCURFIELD, Blaster, Pyeroy
W SEATON, Scaffolder, Tyssen-Krupp Palmers
D SHARPHOUSE, Labourer,
    Tyssen-Krupp Palmers
R SHAW, Blaster, Tyssen-Krupp Palmers
D SHEPHERD, Labourer, Tyssen-Krupp Palmers
T SHERIFF, Scaffolder, Tyssen-Krupp Palmers
J SHERLOCK, Labourer, Vital
J SHIELS, Blaster, Tyssen-Krupp Palmers
J SHIELS, Blaster, Pyeroy
S SHORT, Labourer, Balfour Beatty
M SIM, Labourer, Vital
M SIM, Lookout, Orion
D SIMMONDS, Blaster, Pyeroy
D SIMMONDS, Deck Crew, Pyeroy
I SIMMS, Construction Manager, Network Rail
A SIMPSON, Blaster, Pyeroy
C SIMPSON, EN, SGB
C SIMPSON, Labourer, Balfour Beatty
C SIMPSON, Scaffolder, SGB
G SIMPSON, Labourer, Vital
T SIMPSON, Labourer, Tyssen-Krupp Palmers
T SIMPSON, Trac, Tyssen-Krupp Palmers
D SINCLAIR, EN, SGB
M SINCLAIR, Blaster, Pyeroy
J SKELTON, Labourer, Vital
J SKILLING, Consultant, Balfour Beatty
M SKINNER, Scaffolder, SGB
M SKINNER, Labourer, Tyssen-Krupp Palmers
S SMALL, Labourer, Tyssen-Krupp Palmers
S SMALL, Handler, Tyssen-Krupp Palmers
W SMART, Labourer, Vital
J SMEDLEY, Scaffolder, SGB
J SMEDLEY, Scaffolder, SGB
A SMITH, Scaffolder, Tyssen-Krupp Palmers
C SMITH, Labourer, Vital

C SMITH, Supervisor, SGB
D SMITH, Labourer, Balfour Beatty
D SMITH, Scaffolder, Protec
G SMITH, Labourer, Balfour Beatty
J SMITH, Lookout, Scotweld
J SMITH, Supervisor, Pyeroy
K SMITH, Scaffolder, Tyssen-Krupp Palmers
M SMITH, Abseiler, Tyssen-Krupp Palmers
M SMITH, Blaster, Tyssen-Krupp Palmers
M SMITH, Blaster, Tyssen-Krupp Palmers
M SMITH, Scaffolder, SGB
P SMITH, Abseiler, Pyeroy
P SMITH, Blaster, Tyssen-Krupp Palmers
P SMITH, Deck Crew, Geckotech Solutions Ltd
P SMITH, Deck Crew, Pyeroy
R SMITH, Lookout, Orion
S SMITH, Electrician, Vital
S SMITH, Labourer, Balfour Beatty
S SMITH, Steelworker, Tyssen-Krupp Palmers
J SNEDDON, COSS, Vital
M SNEDDON, Abseiler, Pyeroy
M SNEDDON, Blaster, Tyssen-Krupp Palmers
T SNEDDON, Blaster, Pyeroy
T SNEDDON, Blaster, Pyeroy
I SNOW, Lookout, Orion
B SOMERVILLE, Scaffolder, SGB
C SOMERVILLE, COSS, Vital
J SOMMERVILLE, Supervisor, SGB
D SOOMAN, Head of Engineering, Network Rail
R SOUTAR, Scaffolder, Tyssen-Krupp Palmers
S SOUTER, Labourer, Vital
T SPEARS, Labourer, Vital
G SPENCER, Warden, Vital
L SPOOR, 'Chemist, Site Engineer', WJ Leighs
A STATTERS, Scaffolder, SGB
D STEADMAN, Steelworker,
    Tyssen-Krupp Palmers
D STEEN, Labourer, Tyssen-Krupp Palmers
E STELMASZUC, Scaffolder, SGB
G STENSON, COSS, Vital
E STEPHENSON, Scaffolder,
    Tyssen-Krupp Palmers
R STEPHENSON, Scaffolder,
    Tyssen-Krupp Palmers
D STEVENSON, Programme Manager,
    Network Rail
J STEVENSON, Secretary, Balfour Beatty
P STEVENSON, Abseiler, Tyssen-Krupp Palmers
P STEVENSON, Blaster, Tyssen-Krupp Palmers
D STEWART, Labourer, Tyssen-Krupp Palmers
R STEWART, Labourer, Balfour Beatty
R STEWART, Summer Student, Balfour Beatty
S STEWART, Scaffolder, SGB
R STIRLING, Scaffolder, Tyssen-Krupp Palmers
S STORRIE, Scaffolder, SGB
T STORRIE, Scaffolder, SGB
L STOWE, Deck Crew, Pyeroy
D STRANG, Project Manager, Balfour Beatty
M STUART, COSS, Vital
W STUART, Scaffolder, SGB
I SUTHERLAN, Scaffolder,
    Tyssen-Krupp Palmers
D SUTHERLAND, Commercial Manager,
    Balfour Beatty
D SUTHERLAND, Labourer, Balfour Beatty
I SUTHERLAND, Scaffolder,
    Tyssen-Krupp Palmers
J SUTHERLAND, Scaffolder, SGB
J SUTHERLAND, Scaffolder, SGB
C SWAN, Labourer, Tyssen-Krupp Palmers
I SWAN, Labourer, Balfour Beatty
G SWANSON, Lookout, Vital
J SWEDDON, Labourer, Vital
A SWEENEY, Scaffolder, Pyeroy
S SWEENY, Lookout, Scotweld
K SWIFT, Supervisor, Tyssen-Krupp Palmers
K SWIFT, Supervisor, Tyssen-Krupp Palmers
F SWORD, Blaster, Tyssen-Krupp Palmers
C SYME, Labourer, Vital
K SYME, Scaffolder, Balfour Beatty
M SZWZEPANS, Labourer, Vital
S T CANDLISH, Deck Crew, Pyeroy
S TAGGART, Lookout, Orion
A TAIT, Labourer, Protec
R TAIT, EN, SGB
R TAIT, Labourer, Balfour Beatty
S TAIT, Deck Crew, Geckotech Solutions Ltd
S TAIT, Deck Crew, Pyeroy
L TANNOCK, Labourer, Vital

J TASHWORTH, Labourer, Vital
D TASSIE, Scaffolder, SGB
D TATE, T, Tyssen-Krupp Palmers
A TAYLOR, Blaster, Pyeroy
I TAYLOR, Labourer, Balfour Beatty
J TAYLOR, Labourer, Balfour Beatty
S TAYLOR, Labourer, Vital
E TEIRNEY, Lookout, Vital
B TELFORD, Labourer, Vital
C TELFORD, Labourer, Vital
R TELFORD, Warden, Vital
C TENNANT, Scaffolder, SGB
S TEPHENSON, Labourer, Balfour Beatty
J THOMAS, Blaster, Tyssen-Krupp Palmers
B THOMPSON, Scaffolder, SGB
D THOMPSON, Planner, MacGregors
D THOMPSON, Scaffolder, Pyeroy
E THOMPSON, Labourer, Vital
E THOMPSON, Scaffolder, SGB
J THOMPSON, Deck Crew, Pyeroy
J THOMPSON, Labourer, Balfour Beatty
M THOMPSON, Scaffolder, SGB
N THOMPSON, Programme Director
    [Construction], Network Rail
P THOMPSON, Labourer, Vital
R THOMPSON, Abseiler, Tyssen-Krupp Palmers
S THOMPSON, Labourer, Balfour Beatty
S THOMPSON, Scaffolder, SGB
A THOMSON, Labourer, Vital
A THOMSON, Regional Managing Director,
    Balfour Beatty
A THOMSON, Controller, AB2000
D THOMSON, Labourer, Vital
S THOMSON, Labourer, Balfour Beatty
T THOMSON, Painter, Tyssen-Krupp Palmers
B THORBURN, Lookout, Orion
T THORBURN, Scaffolder, SGB
D THORNTON, EN, SGB
N THURBRON, Inspector, Pyeroy
C TIERNEY, Scaffolder, SGB
M TOBIN, Painter, Tyssen-Krupp Palmers
J TODD, Labourer, Balfour Beatty
P TODD, Labourer, TEPS
C TOOLE, Safety Adviser, Balfour Beatty
G TOPPING, Scaffolder, SGB
C TORRANCE, Scaffolder, SGB
J TOWNSHEND, Chief Engineer, Balfour Beatty
I TRAYNOR, Labourer, Balfour Beatty
J TULLY, Blaster, Pyeroy
J TULLY, Blaster, Tyssen-Krupp Palmers
J TURNBALL, Scaffolder, Tyssen-Krupp Palmers
J TURNBULL, Scaffolder, Tyssen-Krupp Palmers
R TURNBULL, Abseiler, Geckotech Solutions Ltd
R TURNBULL, Blaster, Pyeroy
R TURNER, Lookout, Orion
W TURNER, Scaffolder, SGB
J TYNAN, Welder, MacGregors
T ULLY, Labourer, Balfour Beatty
D VALLANCE, Labourer, Vital
S VALLANCE, Labourer, Vital
R VAN GOOL, Abseiler, Tyssen-Krupp Palmers
R VAN GOOL, Deck Crew, Pyeroy
C VASEY, Scaffolder, Tyssen-Krupp Palmers
M VAUGHAN, Deck Crew, Pyeroy
V VAUGHAN, Deck Crew, Pyeroy
M VICKERS, Steelworker, Tyssen-Krupp Palmers
M W TABASSUM, Lookout, Orion
W WADDELL, Labourer, Tyssen-Krupp Palmers
G WAIN, Scaffolder, SGB
I WALKER, COSS, Vital
J WALKER, Warden, Vital
J WALKER, Planner, MacGregors
J WALKER, Scaffolder, SGB
J WALKER, Steelworker, MacGregors
C WALKERC, EN, SGB
L WALKERL, Scaffolder, SGB
D WALLACE, Labourer, Vital
D WALLACE, Labourer, Vital
J WARD, Scaffolder, Pyeroy
D WARDALE, Scaffolder, Pyeroy
M WARE, Scaffolder, Tyssen-Krupp Palmers
N WATERS, Lookout, Scotweld
J WATERSON, Scaffolder,
    Tyssen-Krupp Palmers
G WATERSTON, Commercial Manager,
    Balfour Beatty
A WATSON, Lookout, Scotweld
G WATSON, Labourer, Balfour Beatty
I WATSON, Deck Crew, Pyeroy

J WATSON, COSS, Vital
M WATSON, Labourer, Tyssen-Krupp Palmers
M WATSON, Scaffolder, Tyssen-Krupp Palmers
N WATSON, Labourer, Balfour Beatty
S WATSON, Painter, Tyssen-Krupp Palmers
D WATT, Labourer, SGB
C WEBSTER, Labourer, Tyssen-Krupp Palmers
S WEDDERBURN, Labourer,
    Tyssen-Krupp Palmers
I WEIR, Scaffolder, Tyssen-Krupp Palmers
A WELDON, Deck Crew, Pyeroy
I WEST WORTH, Deck Crew, Pyeroy
G WHEELEY, Scaffolder,
    Tyssen-Krupp Palmers
S WHIGHAM, Labourer, Balfour Beatty
S WHITE, Scaffolder, SGB
J WHITEFORD, Supervisor, Vital
A WHITEHEAD, Scaffolder, SGB
J WHITEHEAD, Deck Crew, Pyeroy
J WHITEHEAD, EN, SGB
J WHITFEILD, Labourer, Balfour Beatty
D WHYTE, Planner, MacGregors
L WHYTE, Painter, Tyssen-Krupp Palmers
S WHYTE, Scaffolder, SGB
A WICKSTED, Handler, SGB
S WIGHAM, Labourer, Balfour Beatty
P WILKIESON, EN, SGB
B WILLIAMS, EN, SGB
G WILLIAMS, Scaffolder, Tyssen-Krupp Palmers
A WILLIAMSON, Labourer,
    Tyssen-Krupp Palmers
B WILLIAMSON, Planner, MacGregors
G WILLIAMSON, Scaffolder, SGB
G WILLIAMSON, Scaffolder, SGB
L WILLIAMSON, Labourer, Vital
K WILLSON, Scaffolder, SGB
A WILSON, Labourer, Balfour Beatty
A WILSON, Labourer, Vital
C WILSON, Labourer, Balfour Beatty
C WILSON, Scaffolder, Pyeroy
C WILSON, Scaffolder, SGB
D WILSON, Blaster, Tyssen-Krupp Palmers
D WILSON, Scaffolder, Tyssen-Krupp Palmers
D WILSON, Scaffolder, Tyssen-Krupp Palmers
D WILSON, Scaffolder, Tyssen-Krupp Palmers
I WILSON, Supervisor, Tyssen-Krupp Palmers
J WILSON, Communications Manager,
    Network Rail
K WILSON, COSS, Vital
K WILSON, Labourer, SGB
M WILSON, Blaster, Pyeroy
M WILSON, Painter, Tyssen-Krupp Palmers
N WILSON, Labourer, Balfour Beatty
P WILSON, Scaffolder, SGB
S WILSON, Structural Engineer,
    Pell Frischmann
T WILSON, COSS, Vital
K WILSONN, Scaffolder, Pyeroy
C WISEMAN, Scaffolder, Tyssen-Krupp Palmers
P WISHART, Planner, MacGregors
A WOOD, Labourer, Vital
I WOOD, QA Engineer, Balfour Beatty
J WOOD, Labourer, Vital
C WOODS, Trac, Tyssen-Krupp Palmers
G WOODS, Labourer, Vital
I WOODS, Blaster, LINEAR
A WRIGHT, Foreman, Balfour Beatty
R WRIGHT, Controller, Vital
R WRIGHT, Controller, AB2000
S WRIGHT, Scaffolder, SGB
J WYLIE, Steelworker, MacGregors
J WYN, Lookout, Scotweld
A YOUNG, Scaffolder, Tyssen-Krupp Palmers
B YOUNG, Labourer, Tyssen-Krupp Palmers
B YOUNG, Scaffolder, Tyssen-Krupp Palmers
D YOUNG, Scaffolder, SGB
I YOUNG, Labourer, Vital
I YOUNG, Steelworker, Tyssen-Krupp Palmers
J YOUNG, Deck Crew,
    Geckotech Solutions Ltd
J YOUNG, Labourer, Vital
L YOUNG, Scaffolder, Tyssen-Krupp Palmers
M YOUNG, Abseiler, SGB
S YOUNG, Labourer, Tyssen-Krupp Palmers
J YUILL, Scaffolder, Tyssen-Krupp Palmers
R YVANGOOL, Abseiler, Geckotech
    Solutions Ltd
R ZUCCONI, Planning Manager,
    Balfour Beatty

Every effort has been made to include on this list all individuals who have contributed to delivering this project. Due to the scale of the job, this has been a challenging task, so we apologise in advance if anyone's name has been overlooked.